Early Dictionary

Ginny Lapage
Illustrated by Diana Catchpole

This book was presented to

New Milton Junior School
by
Hannah Parr & Marie Horlock.

Introduction

This is the second dictionary of the Book Bus series. It has been devised with the active help of the children and teachers of a primary school who were involved at all the stages of compilation. The children, familiar with the Book Bus reading scheme, made suggestions as to how the words should be defined or explained. The compiler made adjustments to meet their needs.

The Book Bus Dictionaries have been designed to lead children in stages into using more formal dictionaries. This Early Dictionary has been designed to develop dictionary skills with children who have begun to come to grips with reading. It contains 953 entries, which are based on the vocabulary used in the Early phase of Book Bus. The words are defined according to the context in which they are used in the Book Bus books of the Early phase. The derivatives of headwords are given in full as an aid to correct spelling. This includes forms of verbs, plurals of nouns and comparatives and superlatives of adjectives. Italics are used within the definitions for the first appearance of the headword and any derivative of the headword.

Children can look up words that they do not know and extend their vocabulary. The alphabet is printed at the bottom of each page with the appropriate letter highlighted in colour. If the dictionary is used as regular practice children will become skilled in its use and be able to locate words quickly and easily.

Ginny Lapage is an experienced primary school teacher. She has an M. A. in Children's Literature and a Diploma in Reading and Language Development. She has compiled the *Collins Junior Dictionary*, the accompanying workbook and the workbooks for *Collins Picture Dictionary* and *Collins Primary Dictionary*.

How to use this dictionary

A dictionary tells you the meaning of a word and how to spell it.

You will find it easy to look up words in your dictionary if you can say the letters of the alphabet in the right order. You can see them at the bottom of this page and at the bottom of every page in this book.

If you want to find a word you need to think about the letter the word begins with. If you wanted to look up **pirate** you would turn the pages until you come to the letter **p**. There are lots of **p** words. How can you find **pirate** without looking at every one? Look at the second letter of **pirate**. It is **i**. Keep looking through the pages until you come to the words beginning with **pi** and you will find **pirate**.

As you get used to looking up words in the dictionary, you will find that you can do it much more quickly!

actor
(actors)

A person or animal that performs in a play or film is called an *actor*. A woman or girl who performs in a play or a film is called an *actress*.

aeroplane
(aeroplanes)

An *aeroplane* is a machine that flies. It can carry passengers or goods.

air

Air is all around you but you cannot see it. You need air to breathe.

alien
(aliens)

An *alien* is a creature that comes from another planet.

alive

1. If something is *alive*, it is not dead.
2. If something or someone *comes alive*, they seem to wake up.

alley
(alleys)

An *alley* is a narrow street or passageway between buildings.

alligator
(alligators)

An *alligator* is like a crocodile but it has a shorter and broader jaw and bigger teeth. *Alligators* live in lakes and rivers in America and China.

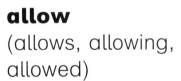

allow
(allows, allowing, allowed)

If you *allow* someone to do something, you let them do it.

amazing

If something is *amazing*, it is surprising and unusual.

ancient

Something that is *ancient* is very, very old.

angry

If you are *angry*, someone or something has made you upset and cross.

animal
(animals)

All living things, except plants, are *animals*.

answer
(answers, answering, answered)

When you *answer* someone, you say something to them in reply to something they have said.

ant
(ants)

An *ant* is a tiny insect. *Ants* live underground in large groups called colonies.

ape
(apes)

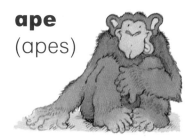

An *ape* is a large monkey with a very short or no tail. Chimpanzees, orang-outans and gibbons are all *apes*.

appear
(appears, appearing, appeared)

If someone *appears* on the television, in an advertisement, a play or a film, they take part in it.

apple
(apples)

An *apple* is a crisp, round fruit which grows on a tree. It is usually red, yellow or green and it has pips. You can eat it raw or cooked.

area
(areas)

An *area* is a flat part of a space or surface of something.

arm
(arms)

Your *arm* is the part of your body which is joined to your shoulder.

armour

Armour is special clothing, usually made of metal, that is worn for protection.

arrive
(arrives, arriving, arrived)

If you *arrive* somewhere, you get there. Your *arrival* is the moment that you get there.

ask
(asks, asking, asked)

If you *ask* someone something, you want to know the answer to a question.

asleep

If you are *asleep*, your eyes are closed and you are not awake.

assistant
(assistants)

An *assistant* is someone who helps other people to do something.

ate

see eat

aunt
(aunts)

Your *aunt* is your mother or father's sister. You might call her *auntie* or *aunty*.

awake

When you are *awake*, your eyes are open and you know what is going on around you.

awful

If something is *awful*, it is very bad, ugly or nasty.

IT'S AWFUL!

a b c d e f g h i j k l m

Bb

baby
(babies)

A *baby* is a child or animal that has just been born.

back
(backs)

1. The *back* of something is behind not in front.
2. If you *come back* or *get back* from somewhere, you return to the place where you began.
3. If you *put* something *back*, you put it in the place where you found it.

bad
(worse, worst)

If you are *bad*, you are naughty.

bag
(bags)

A *bag* holds or carries things. It is open at the top and can be made of paper, leather, cloth or plastic.

bake
(bakes, baking, baked)

If you *bake* something, you cook it in an oven. A *baker* works in a bakery.

ball
(balls)

A *ball* is a round object that you use for games. It can be soft or hard, large or small.

balloon
(balloons)

A *balloon* is a small, brightly coloured bag of thin rubber that you can blow up.

banana
(bananas)

A *banana* is a long, thin, curved fruit with a thick yellow skin.

bang
(bangs, banging, banged)

1. A *bang* is a sudden loud explosion or noise.
2. If two things *bang* together, they hit each other hard.

bark
(barks, barking, barked)

When a dog *barks*, it makes a short, loud sound.

a **b** c d e f g h i j k l m

bash
(bashes,
bashing, bashed)

If you *bash* something, you hit it very hard.

basket
(baskets)

A *basket* is a bag made of canes or thin strips of wood. It is open at the top and has a handle.

bat
(bats, batting,
batted)

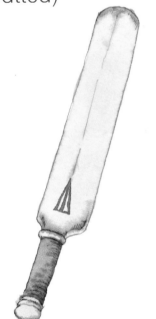

1. A *bat* is a small animal, like a mouse with wings.
2. A *bat* is a piece of wood you use for hitting a ball in a game.

3. If you *bat* in a game of cricket, you take your turn at hitting the ball.

battle
(battles)

A *battle* is a fight in a war between ships, armies or aeroplanes.

n o p q r s t u v w x y z

beach
(beaches)

A *beach* is a long stretch of sand or pebbles beside the sea or a lake.

bean
(beans)

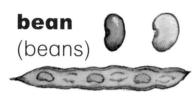

A *bean* is a vegetable that grows inside long pods like *broad beans*, *runner beans* and *kidney beans*.

bear
(bears)

1. A *bear* is a large, strong, wild animal with thick fur and sharp claws. *Bears* live in cool countries and some can be very dangerous.
2. A *bear* is a soft toy usually called a *teddy bear*.

beautiful

If someone or something is *beautiful,* they are very pretty or attractive.

bed
(beds)

A *bed* is a piece of furniture to sleep on. It is kept in the *bedroom*.

bee
(bees)

A *bee* is a small flying insect. It has black and yellow stripes and can make honey. Honey *bees* live in a *beehive*.

a **b** c d e f g h i j k l m

beg
(begs, begging, begged)

If someone *begs*, they ask someone again and again for something.

begin
(begins, beginning, began, begun)

When you *begin* something, you start it.

believe
(believes, believing, believed)

If you *believe* something, you are sure it is true.

bell
(bells)

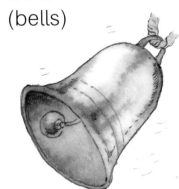

A *bell* is a hollow piece of metal which rings when you strike it. *Church bells* are huge and ring when you pull a long rope. A bell on a front or back door rings inside the house when you press a button. This type of bell works by electricity.

bicycle
(bicycles)

A *bicycle* has two wheels and two pedals. You move the pedals to make the wheels go round. A bicycle is also called a *bike*.

big
(bigger, biggest)

If something is *big*, it is large.

bin
(bins)

A *bin* is a container for rubbish.

bird
(birds)

A *bird* is a creature with two legs, two wings and is covered with feathers. Most *birds* can fly. The young are hatched from eggs.

birthday
(birthdays)

Your *birthday* is the special day that you celebrate every year because it is the day you were born.

biscuit
(biscuits)

A *biscuit* is a crisp, thin cake. It can be sweet or savoury.

bit
(bits)

A *bit* is a small piece or amount of something.

a **b** c d e f g h i j k l m

bite
(bites, biting, bit, bitten)

When you *bite* something, you close your teeth on it to break it.

block
(blocks)

A *block* of flats or offices is a tall building where many people live or work.

blood

Blood is the red liquid that your heart pumps around your body.

blow
(blows, blowing, blew, blown)

1. If you *blow*, you make air come out of your mouth.
2. When the wind *blows*, everything is moved by it.

boat
(boats)

A *boat* is a small ship that can take people and goods over water.

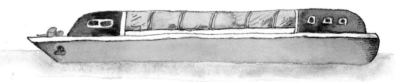

body
(bodies)

Your *body* is the whole of you.

boil
(boils, boiling, boiled)

If you *boil* water, milk or any other liquid, you heat it until it bubbles and steams and is very hot.

bomb
(bombs)

A *bomb* is a weapon that explodes and does a lot of damage.

bone
(bones)

The hard parts of your body are made of *bone*. All your *bones* together make your skeleton.

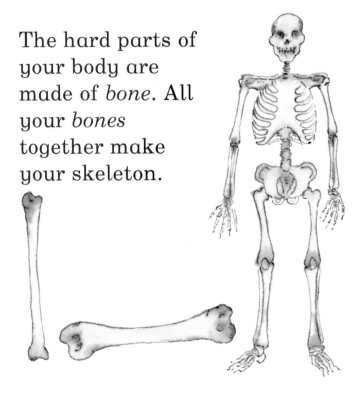

book
(books)

A *book* is made of many pages of paper fixed together inside a cover.

boom
(booms)

A *boom* is a very loud, deep noise.

a **b** c d e f g h i j k l m

boot
(boots, booting, booted)

1. A *boot* covers your foot, ankle and sometimes your leg up to your knee.
2. The *boot* of a car is the space with no seats where you can put cases, shopping or other large things.
3. If you *boot* a ball, you kick it hard.

bored

If you are *bored*, you feel tired and fed up because you are not interested in doing anything.

bottle
(bottles)

A *bottle* is a container for storing liquids. It is usually narrow at the top. Some bottles are made of glass or plastic and hold cold liquids like milk or juice. Some *bottles*, like *hot water bottles*, are specially made of rubber to hold hot liquids.

bottom
(bottoms)

The *bottom* of something is the lowest part.

bought

see buy

bounce
(bounces,
bouncing,
bounced)

If you *bounce* a ball, you hit it against something hard and it springs back. Something *bouncy* is springy.

bowl
(bowls)

A *bowl* is a round, deep dish for liquid or food.

box
(boxes)

A *box* is a container with flat or rounded sides. It may have a lid.

boy
(boys)

A *boy* is a male child.

branch
(branches)

A *branch* is a part of a tree that grows out from its trunk like an arm.

a **b** c d e f g h i j k l m

brawl
(brawls)

If there is a *brawl*, many people fight each other with their fists or struggle roughly.

bread

Bread is a food made of flour, water and, often, yeast.

break
(breaks, breaking, broke, broken)

If you *break* something, it splits into pieces or stops working.

breakfast
(breakfasts)

Breakfast is the meal you eat when you get up in the morning. It is the first meal of the day.

breed
(breeds, breeding, bred)

1. A *breed* of an animal is a particular type of animal.

2. If you *breed* animals, you keep them to get young from them.

brewery
(breweries)

A *brewery* is a place where beer is made. A brewery is also the name of a company that makes beer.

brick
(bricks)

A *brick* is a rectangular block used for making buildings.

bright
(brighter,
brightest)

If something is *bright*, it shines strongly.

brilliant

If you are *brilliant* at something, you are very, very good at it.

bring
(brings, bringing,
brought)

If you *bring* something to a place, it comes with you when you go there.

broom
(brooms)

A *broom* is a type of brush for sweeping the floor.

a **b** c d e f g h i j k l m

brother
(brothers)

Your *brother* is a boy who has the same mother and father as you.

brought

see bring

brush
(brushes,
brushing,
brushed)

1. A *brush* is an object made of wood, plastic, or metal with bristles fixed to it. There are many different sizes and uses for *brushes*.
2. If you *brush* something, such as your hair or an animal's fur, you use a brush to tidy it.

bubble
(bubbles)

A *bubble* is a ball of air inside a thin film of liquid.

build
(builds, building, built)

If you *build* something, you join things together to make it. A *builder* joins bricks together to make a *building*.

bull
(bulls)

A *bull* is a male animal of the cow family.

bungalow
(bungalows)

A *bungalow* is a house built only on one level.

burger
(burgers)

A *burger* is a bun filled with a flat, round piece of minced beef and, sometimes, onions.

burglar
(burglars)

A *burglar* is a thief who breaks into houses and steals things.

burn
(burns, burning, burned or burnt)

1. If you *burn* fuel, such as coal or wood, you make a fire.
2. If something hot *burns* you, it hurts you with the heat.
3. An engine *burns* oil to make it work.

burp
(burps, burping, burped)

If someone *burps*, they make a noise when air comes up through their throat from their stomach.

bury
(buries, burying, buried)

If you *bury* something, you dig a hole, put it into the ground and cover it over again with earth.

bus
(buses)

A *bus* is a large vehicle for taking many people from one place to another.

a b c d e f g h i j k l m

bush
(bushes)

A *bush* is a large woody plant with lots of branches.

busy
(busier, busiest)

If you are *busy*, you are working hard at something and have no time to do anything else.

butterfly
(butterflies)

A *butterfly* is an insect with four large wings. It begins life as an egg, hatches out into a caterpillar, then spins a cocoon around itself and later comes out as a butterfly.

button
(buttons)

A *button* is small and round with holes in the middle so it can be sewn onto cloth. *Buttons* are used to hold clothes together and they are usually made of plastic or wood.

buy
(buys, buying, bought)

If you *buy* something, you pay money to get it.

buzz
(buzzes, buzzing, buzzed)

If something *buzzes*, it makes a noise that sounds like a bee.

café
(cafés)

A *café* is a place where you can buy a cup of tea or coffee and snacks.

cake
(cakes)

A *cake* is a sweet food usually made from eggs, flour, sugar and margarine and baked in an oven.

calendar
(calendars)

A *calendar* is a list which shows all the days of the week and the months of the year.

call
(calls, calling, called)

1. If you *call*, you speak loudly.
2. If you *call* someone something, you give them a name.
3. If you *call* someone, you tell them to come to you.

a b **c** d e f g h i j k l m

camel
(camels)

A *camel* is a large animal with one or two humps on its back. *Camels* are used instead of horses in deserts as they can travel a long way without eating or drinking.

canal
(canals)

A *canal* is a man-made river. It is usually straight.

car
(cars)

A *car* is a machine with four wheels and an engine that carries passengers by road.

cardboard

Very thick, strong paper is called *cardboard.* It is used to make things like boxes.

cardigan
(cardigans)

A *cardigan* is a knitted jacket that has buttons.

care
(cares, caring, cared)

1. If you *care* about someone, they are important to you and you like them.
2. If you *take care* of someone, you look after him or her.
3. If you *take care* when you hold or touch something, you are *careful* not to damage it.
4. If you say *'Take care'*, you tell someone to look after himself or herself.

caretaker
(caretakers)

A *caretaker* looks after a building as a job.

carpet
(carpets)

A *carpet* is a floor covering which is usually made of something like wool.

carriage
(carriages)

A *carriage* is a horse-drawn vehicle with four wheels.

a b c d e f g h i j k l m

carry
(carries,
carrying, carried)

If you *carry* something, you lift it up and take it from one place to another.

cart
(carts)

A *cart* is a small vehicle on wheels that you can pull or push. Sometimes horses or cattle pull *carts*, especially on farms.

castle
(castles)

A *castle* is a very big, old building with very thick walls. *Castles* were built many years ago to protect the people living inside from their enemies.

cat
(cats)

A *cat* is a mammal. Often small *cats* are kept as pets. Larger cats, like lions and tigers, live in the wild.

catch
(catches,
catching, caught)

1. If you *catch* something, like a ball, you take hold of it when it comes towards you through the air.
2. If you *catch* an animal, you trap it.
3. If the police *catch* criminals, they take them to the police station.
4. If you *catch* a cold, you sneeze, your nose runs and you feel ill.
5. If you *catch* a train, you get on it to go somewhere.

caterpillar
(caterpillars)

A *caterpillar* is a small creature, like a worm, with legs. It can be many different colours. It grows into a butterfly or a moth.

cattle

Cattle are cows and bulls which are kept on a farm.

a b c d e f g h i j k l m

caught   see catch

centre
(centres)

1. The *centre* of something is the middle of it.
2. A *centre* for something is the main place where something, like shopping or sport, happens.

cereal
(cereals)

1. *Cereals* are crops that farmers grow for seed. Oats, barley and wheat are cereals.
2. *Cereal* is a food made from the seed of cereal plants that you eat for breakfast.

chair
(chairs)

A *chair* is a seat for one person.

champion
(champions)

The *champion* is the winner of a competition. *Champ* is short for champion.

change
(changes, changing, changed)

When something *changes*, it becomes different.

channel
(channels)

A *channel* is a narrow stretch of water between two pieces of land.

chariot
(chariots)

A *chariot* is a small cart with two wheels pulled by horses. Long ago, *chariots* were used for fighting and racing contests.

chase
(chases, chasing, chased)

If you *chase* someone or something, you run after them and try to catch them.

chat
(chats, chatting, chatted)

If you *chat* to someone, you talk about things that are not very important in a friendly way.

cheese
(cheeses)

Cheese is a food made from milk which has been stirred until it is thick. Then the liquid is squeezed out of it and the solid part left behind is called cheese.

a b c d e f g h i j k l m

chest of drawers
(chests of drawers)

A *chest of drawers* is a piece of furniture used for storing clothes.

child
(children)

A *child* is a young boy or girl.

choose
(chooses, choosing, chose, chosen)

If you *choose* something, you pick out the one you want. You make a *choice*.

chose

see choose

Christmas
(Christmases)

Christmas is the time of year when Christians celebrate Jesus Christ's birthday. *Christmas day* is on 25th December.

church
(churches)

A *church* is a building where people pray to God.

circle
(circles)

A *circle* is a curved line with both ends joined. It makes the shape of a ring.

circus
(circuses)

A *circus* is a show held in a tent called a Big Top. Acrobats, clowns and jugglers all perform tricks to entertain the people who come to watch.

city
(cities)

A *city* is a very big and busy town.

class
(classes)

A *class* is a group of children who have lessons together in school.

a b c d e f g h i j k l m

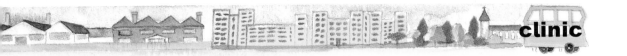

clatter

If you make a *clatter*, you make short, loud noises one after the other.

clean
(cleans, cleaning, cleaned)

If you *clean* something, you take away the dirt.

clear
(clears, clearing, cleared)

If you *clear* things away, you tidy up.

climb
(climbs, climbing, climbed)

If you *climb* a hill or a ladder, you go up it. A *mountain climber climbs* up mountains.

clinic
(clinics)

A *clinic* is a place, often in a hospital, where people go to get advice about their health.

n o p q r s t u v w x y z

clock
(clocks)

A *clock* is a machine that measures time.

close
(closer, closest)

If you are *close* to something, you are near to it.

clothes

Clothes are things you wear to cover your body.

cloud
(clouds)

A *cloud* is a patch of white or grey that floats in the sky. *Clouds* are made of many tiny drops of water which sometimes fall as rain.

coach
(coaches)

A *coach* is a carriage pulled by horses. A *coaching inn* was a place where people used to stop for refreshment.

a b c d e f g h i j k l m

coal

Coal is hard, black rock that is dug out from under the ground. It is burned to give heat.

coast
(coasts)

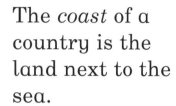

The *coast* of a country is the land next to the sea.

coat
(coats)

A *coat* is a piece of clothing with long sleeves that you wear over the top of your other clothes.

coat-of-arms
(coats-of-arms)

A *coat-of-arms* is a special design that belongs to a family, a town or city, or to a particular group of people. *Coats-of-arms* are usually found on shields.

cockatoo
(cockatoos)

A *cockatoo* is a parrot that comes from Australia. It has a crest on its head.

coin
(coins)

A *coin* is a piece of metal money.

cold
(colder, coldest)

1. If the weather is *cold*, the temperature outside is low.
2. If something is *cold*, it is not hot or warm.

collect
(collects,
collecting,
collected)

1. If you *collect* something, you go and fetch it from another place. Some people collect things as their job, such as a *ticket collector*.
2. If you *collect* special things like stamps, thimbles, model cars or books and keep them together in a *collection*, you are a *collector*.

colour
(colours,
colouring,
coloured)

1. Red, blue and green are *colours*.
2. If you *colour* something, you use crayons or paints on it.
3. If something is *coloured*, it is a particular colour.

a b c d e f g h i j k l m

contents

The *contents* of something, like a box or a bag, is what is inside it.

contrary

If you are *contrary*, you are bad-tempered.

control
(controls, controlling, controlled)

If you *control* something, you are in charge of it and make it do what you want.

cook
(cooks, cooking, cooked)

If you *cook* food, you heat it before you eat it. Boiling, frying, baking, roasting, grilling and steaming are all ways of *cooking* food.

cool
(cooler, coolest)

If something is *cool*, it is not hot or cold.

corner
(corners)

A *corner* is the place where two edges, two streets or two walls meet.

cottage
(cottages)

A *cottage* is a small house, usually in the country.

cotton

1. *Cotton* is a thread used for sewing.
2. *Cotton* is a light material used for making clothes.
3. *Cotton* is a plant that is grown in hot countries. The soft fibres around its seeds are used to make thread and material.

count
(counts,
counting,
counted)

1. When you *count*, you say numbers in order: one, two, three...
2. If you *count* people, animals or objects, you add them up to see how many there are.

country
(countries)

1. The *country* is a place away from towns where there are fields, woods and rivers. It is also called the *countryside*.

2. A *country* is a place which has its own people and laws.

a b c d e f g h i j k l m

course
(courses)

The *course* of something is the way it goes. The course of a river is the path it takes. A *race course* is the place where races are held.

cousin
(cousins)

Your *cousin* is the child of your aunt or uncle.

cow
(cows)

A *cow* is a large farm animal that gives milk.

cowboy
(cowboys)

In America, a *cowboy* rides on a horse to look after a large herd of cattle.

crab
(crabs)

A *crab* is a sea animal with a hard shell, two large claws and eight legs.

crack
(cracks,
cracking,
cracked)

1. A *crack* is a thin opening where something has been partly broken.

2. If something *cracks*, it breaks without falling apart completely.

crane
(cranes)

A *crane* is a machine that moves very heavy things.

crash
(crashes)

A *crash* is a sudden, loud, breaking sound.

crawl
(crawls, crawling, crawled)

If you *crawl*, you move along on your hands and knees.

cream

Cream is the thick fatty layer on top of milk.

creep
(creeps, creeping, crept)

If you *creep*, you move slowly and quietly.

cricket

Cricket is a game played by two teams in a field. They use a ball, two bats and two wickets.

crops

Crops are plants such as corn or vegetables that are grown on farms for food.

cross
(crosses)

A *cross* is a monument. It could be a special sign to remember people who gave their lives for their country in a war.

a b **c** d e f g h i j k l m

crowd
(crowds)

A *crowd* is a large number of people gathered together.

crown
(crowns,
crowning,
crowned)

1. A *crown* is the ring of silver or gold that a king or queen wears on their head.
2. If someone is *crowned*, they are made king or queen.

crunch
(crunches,
crunching,
crunched)

If you *crunch* something hard, you crush it noisily between your back teeth.

cry
(cries, crying,
cried)

If you *cry*, you are sad and tears fall from your eyes.

cuddle
(cuddles,
cuddling,
cuddled)

If you *cuddle* someone, you put your arms around them and hold them to show that you love them.

cup
(cups)

A *cup* is a small container with a handle used for drinking liquids.

cupboard
(cupboards)

A *cupboard* is a piece of furniture or a space inside a wall with shelves and space for storing things.

curl
(curls, curling, curled)

1. If your hair is *curly*, it has soft twists in it.

2. If a person or animal *curls up*, they make themselves into a little ball.

curtain
(curtains)

A *curtain* is a covering for a window. It is made of gathered material and hangs from a rail.

customer
(customers)

A *customer* is a person who uses a shop or a bank.

cut
(cuts, cutting, cut)

If you *cut* something, you use something sharp like a knife or a pair of scissors to divide it.

cycle
(cycles)

A *cycle* is a name for a bicycle.

a b **c** **d** e f g h i j k l m

Dd

daddy
(daddies)

Dad and *daddy* are family names for father.

danger
(dangers)

Danger is something that might hurt or harm you.

dark
(darker, darkest)

If it is *dark*, there is no light.

dawn

Dawn is the first light of the day. It is the time when the sun rises.

day
(days)

Day is when it is light and you can see. It begins when the sun comes up and ends when the sun goes down. It is when it is not night.

daydream
(daydreams)

You have a *daydream* when you think about all sorts of lovely things that you would like to happen.

dead

Something that is *dead* is not alive.

dear

If you say *'Oh dear!'*, you are surprised, sad or disappointed about something.

decide
(decides,
deciding,
decided)

If you *decide* something, you make up your mind about it.

deep
(deeper,
deepest)

If something is *deep*, it goes a long way down.

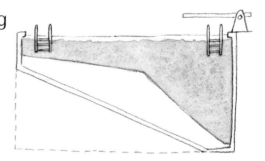

delicious

Something *delicious* tastes or smells very good.

a b c **d** e f g h i j k l m

delighted

If you are *delighted* about something, you are very pleased about it.

deliver
(delivers,
delivering,
delivered)

If you *deliver* something to someone's house, you take it there. If you make a *delivery*, you deliver something.

demon
(demons)

A *demon* is a bad spirit.

desert
(deserts)

A *desert* is dry, sandy or stony land where there is not much water and few plants can grow.

different

If things are *different*, they are not the same.

n o p q r s t u v w x y z

dig
(digs, digging, dug)

When you *dig,* you move soil away to make a hole in the ground with something like a spade. When an animal *digs,* it uses its claws to make a hole.

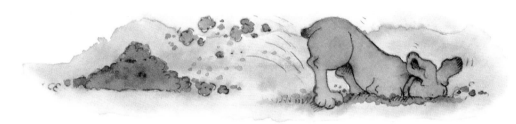

dinner
(dinners)

Dinner is the main meal of the day. It is sometimes eaten at midday and sometimes in the evening.

dinosaur
(dinosaurs)

A *dinosaur* was a large animal that lived on Earth in prehistoric times.

direction
(directions)

The *direction* is the way you go to get somewhere.

dirt

Dirt is dust or mud.

disabled

Someone who is *disabled* has an illness or injury that stops them from moving about easily.

a b c **d** e f g h i j k l m

discover
(discovers,
discovering,
discovered)

If you *discover* something you did not know before, you find out about it.

dish
(dishes)

A *dish* is a shallow bowl for food.

distance
(distances)

The *distance* between two places is the amount of space between them.

dive
(dives, diving,
dived)

If you *dive* into water, you jump in headfirst, with your arms stretched out in front of you.

doctor
(doctors)

A *doctor* is a person whose job is to help people to be well when they are ill.

dog
(dogs)

A *dog* is a four-legged animal that people keep as pets, guards or for hunting.

door
(doors)

A *door* is a piece of wood, glass or metal which is used to close the way in to a building, a room or a cupboard.

doorbell
(doorbells)

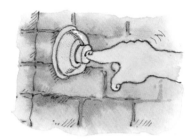

A *doorbell* is a bell on the outside of a house. You ring it to let the people inside know that you are there.

draw
(draws, drawing, drew, drawn)

1. When you *draw*, you make a picture with pencils or crayons.
2. If a horse *draws* a cart, it pulls it along.

dream
(dreams, dreaming, dreamed or dreamt)

You *dream* when you hear sounds and see pictures while you are asleep.

dress
(dresses, dressing, dressed)

1. A *dress* is a piece of clothing that is like a skirt and top joined together.
2. When you *dress*, you put your clothes on.

a b c **d** e f g h i j k l m

drink
(drinks, drinking,
drank, drunk)

1. If you *drink* something, you swallow something liquid, like water.

2. A *drink* is a liquid that is safe to swallow.

drive
(drives, driving,
drove, driven)

If you *drive* a machine or an animal, you make it move along. The person who *drives* is called a *driver*.

drop
(drops, dropping,
dropped)

If you *drop* something, you let it fall to the ground.

drove

see drive

drown
(drowns,
drowning,
drowned)

If you *drown*, you die because you cannot breathe under water.

drum
(drums,
drumming,
drummed)

A *drum* is a musical instrument that you bang with your hands or with sticks.

dry
(drier, driest)

Something that is *dry* is not wet.

duck
(ducks)

A *duck* is a bird that can swim and fly. It has a wide, flat beak.

dug

see dig

dusk

Dusk is the time of day when the sun sets and it begins to get dark.

a b c **d e** f g h i j k l m

Ee

early
(earlier, earliest)

Early is not late. If you arrive somewhere early, you get there before the time that you are expected.

earth

1. *Earth* is the ground where things grow. It is another name for soil.
2. The *Earth* is the name of the planet where we live.

earthquake
(earthquakes)

An *earthquake* is a time when the ground shakes. Sometimes the shaking is so bad that buildings fall down.

eat
(eats, eating, ate, eaten)

If you *eat*, you take food into your body.

egg
(eggs)

An *egg* is an oval or round object laid by birds, snakes, fish or insects. The young hatch from the *eggs* after a little time.

elephant
(elephants)

An *elephant* is the biggest animal that lives on land. It has a long nose, called a trunk, and tusks.

empty
(empties,
emptying,
emptied)

1. If you *empty* something, you take everything out of it.
2. When something is *empty*, it has nothing in it.

end
(ends, ending,
ended)

1. The *end* of something is when it finishes.
2. The *end* is the last part of something.
3. If you *end* something, you finish it off.
4. If a film or a television programme *ends*, it stops.

energy
(energies)

Energy is the strength to do things.

a b c d e f g h i j k l m

engine
(engines)

An *engine* is a machine that makes its own power and is used to make things move.

engineer
(engineers)

An *engineer* is someone who plans how roads, bridges or machines will be built.

enjoy
(enjoys, enjoying, enjoyed)

If you *enjoy* doing something, you are happy while you are doing it.

enormous

Enormous things are very, very large.

eskimo
(eskimos)

An *Eskimo* is one of the people who live in the very cold parts of North America, Greenland and Russia. The *Eskimos* are also called Innuit.

event
(events)

An *event* is something important that happens.

eye
(eyes)

The *eyes* of a person or an animal are the parts they use to see with.

n o p q r s t u v w x y z

face
(faces, facing, faced)

1. Your *face* is the front part of your head where your eyes, mouth and nose are.
2. If you *face* something difficult, you are brave about it.
3. The *face* in a mine is the part where the miners cut the coal or metal from.

fact
(facts)

A *fact* is something that is true.

factory
(factories)

A *factory* is a building where goods are made by machines.

fall
(falls, falling, fell, fallen)

If you *fall*, you come down or drop to the ground suddenly.

a b c d e **f** g h i j k l m

family
(families)

A *family* is a group of people who are related and, usually, live together and care for each other. There is usually a mother, a father and children.

famous

If someone is *famous*, he or she is very well-known.

fantastic

If something is *fantastic*, it is very wonderful and surprising.

far
(farther, farthest)

If a place is a long way away, it is *far*.

farm
(farms)

A *farm* is a large area of land where the *farmer* keeps animals and grows crops like corn and vegetables. A farm has buildings for the farmer to live in and barns for storing crops and sheltering the animals. The *farmyard* is the outdoor area around the *farmhouse*.

n o p q r s t u v w x y z

fast
(faster, fastest)

If something is *fast*, it moves very quickly.

fat
(fatter, fattest)

If a person or animal is *fat*, they are very big and have a lot of flesh on their body.

father
(fathers)

A *father* is a man who has his own child or children.

favourite

Your *favourite* thing is the one you like the best.

feather
(feathers)

A *feather* is one of the many very light pieces that make up the covering of a bird's body.

feed
(feeds, feeding, fed)

When you *feed* someone, you give them something to eat.

a b c d e **f** g h i j k l m

feel
(feels, feeling, felt)

If you *feel* sad, happy or ill, that is the way you are at the time.

feet

see foot

fell

see fall

felt

see feel

female
(females)

Any person or animal that is *female* can have babies.

fence
(fences)

A *fence* is something that divides two pieces of land. It can be made of wire or of wood.

ferry
(ferries)

A *ferry* is a boat that takes people and cars across a stretch of water. The *ferryman* operates it.

fetch
(fetches,
fetching, fetched)

When you *fetch* something, you go and get it.

fête
(fêtes)

A *fête* is a kind of open-air party with competitions and stalls selling cakes, toys and many other things.

few
(fewer, fewest)

If you have a *few* things, you do not have very many.

fibre
(fibres)

A *fibre* is a thin thread of something like wool, cotton or nylon.

fiddle
(fiddles)

A *fiddle* is another name for a violin. Someone who plays a fiddle is called a *fiddler*.

a b c d e **f** g h i j k l m

field
(fields)

A *field* is a piece of land with a fence or a hedge around it.

fight
(fights, fighting, fought)

1. When people or animals *fight*, they try to hurt each other.
2. If you *fight* an illness, you try to get better.

fill
(fills, filling, filled)

If you *fill* something, you put so much in that there is no room for more. It is *full*.

film
(films)

A *film* is moving pictures which tell a story and are shown on a screen. Well-known people or animals who appear in films are called *film stars*.

finally

If someone *finally* does something, they do it after a long time.

find
(finds, finding, found)

If you *find* something, you see it or come across it after you have been looking for it.

fine
(finer, finest)

If something is *fine*, it is very good indeed.

finger
(fingers)

Your *finger* is one of the five separate parts at the end of your hand.

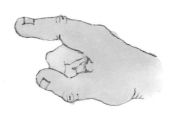

fire
(fires)

Fire is the bright light and heat from something burning. If your home is *on fire*, a *fire engine* from the *fire station* will bring *fire fighters* to put it out.

a b c d e **f** g h i j k l m

fish
(fish or fishes)

A *fish* is a creature with scales and fins that lives under water and breathes through gills. People who catch fish for their job or for sport are called *fishermen*.

flap
(flaps, flapping, flapped)

If a bird *flaps* its wings, it makes them move up and down.

flash
(flashes, flashing, flashed)

1. A *flash* is a sudden bright light that lasts for just a moment, like a *flash* of lightning.
2. If something happens *in a flash*, it happens very quickly.

flat
(flats, flatter, flattest)

1. If something is *flat*, it has no bumps in it.
2. A *flat* is a group of rooms on one floor in a large building for people to live in.

flew

see fly

float
(floats, floating, floated)

If something *floats*, it rests on the top of a liquid.

n o p q r s t u v w x y z

flock
(flocks)

A *flock* is a group of sheep or birds gathered together.

flood
(floods)

A *flood* is a huge amount of water that spreads over a large area of land, which is usually dry.

floor
(floors)

The *floor* is the flat part of a room that people walk on.

flour

Flour is a white or brown powder made from grinding grain such as wheat. Flour is used to make food such as bread and cakes.

flower
(flowers)

1. A *flower* is the part of a plant that holds seeds. It is usually brightly coloured and lasts for a short time.
2. When a plant or tree *flowers*, its buds open.

a b c d e **f** g h i j k l m

fluff

Fluff is light, soft stuff that comes off wool, cotton, fur and hair. If something is *fluffy*, it is soft and woolly.

flutter
(flutters, fluttering, fluttered)

If a bird or insect *flutters*, it flaps its wings very quickly as it flies through the air.

fly
(flies, flying, flew, flown)

1. A *fly* is a small insect with one pair of wings.
2. If a bird or a plane *flies*, it travels through the air.

follow
(follows, following, followed)

1. If you *follow* something, you go after it.
2. If you *follow* a path, you go along it.

food
(food or foods)

Food is what we eat to help us grow.

foot
(feet)

Your *foot* is part of your body. It joins your leg at your ankle. If you make a mark on something with your foot, you make a *footprint*.

football
(footballs)

1. *Football* is a game that is played by two teams. They try to score goals by kicking a ball into a net.

2. A *football* is the name of the ball that is used for playing the game of football.

forget
(forgets, forgetting, forgot, forgotten)

When you *forget* something, you do not remember it even though you knew it before.

found

see find

foundations

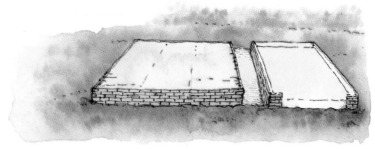

The *foundations* of a building are the solid parts underground that stop it falling down.

a b c d e **f** g h i j k l m

fox
(foxes)

A *fox* is a wild animal which looks like a dog. It has reddish-brown fur and a bushy tail.

free

1. If you are *free*, there is nothing to stop you from doing anything you want to do.
2. If something is *free,* you do not have to pay for it.

fresh
(fresher, freshest)

If something is *fresh*, it is new.

friend
(friends)

A *friend* is someone you like and who likes you too. If someone is *friendly*, they behave in a kind and pleasant way to other people.

frighten
(frightens,
frightening,
frightened)

If you *frighten* someone, you make them feel afraid.

frog
(frogs)

A *frog* is a small animal with smooth skin, big eyes and long back legs which it uses for jumping. *Frogs* live near water.

front

The *front* of someone or something is the side that people usually see first. It is the part that faces you.

fruit
(fruit or fruits)

Fruit is the part of a tree or plant that holds the seeds. You can eat the juicy part around the seeds or the stone.

fry
(fries, frying, fried)

If you *fry* food, you cook it in a pan with hot fat.

full
(fuller, fullest)

If something is *full,* there is no room for anything else to fit in.

fun

Having *fun* is enjoying yourself and doing things that make you happy.

funny
(funnier, funniest)

Funny things are amusing and make you laugh.

furniture

Furniture means things like beds, tables, chairs and cupboards that you need in a house and that you can move about.

a b c d e **f g** h i j k l m

Gg

game
(games)

1. A *game* is something you play for fun. You can play with toys or you can pretend to be someone else.
2. A *game* is a sport that you play with rules. You use your skill to try to win.

garden
(gardens)

A *garden* is land next to someone's house where they can grow flowers, trees and vegetables. A person who looks after a garden as a job is called a *gardener*.

gate
(gates)

A *gate* is like a door in a fence or a wall.

gentle
(gentler, gentlest)

If something is *gentle,* it is soft, quiet and light. If you touch something or someone *gently,* you touch them softly.

gentleman
(gentlemen)

A *gentleman* is a polite name for a man.

giant
(giants)

In fairy stories, a *giant* is a huge person.

girl
(girls)

A *girl* is a female child.

give
(gives, giving,
gave, given)

If you *give* someone something, you let them have it.

gleam
(gleams,
gleaming,
gleamed)

When something *gleams,* it shines.

a b c d e f **g** h i j k l m

gloomy
(gloomier,
gloomiest)

1. When the weather is *gloomy*, it is cloudy and dark.

2. If you feel *gloomy*, you feel sad.

glossary
(glossaries)

A *glossary* is an alphabetical list of words with their meanings that you find at the back of a book.

gloves

Gloves are coverings for your hands to protect them or to keep them warm.

good
(better, best)

1. If a child or animal is *good*, they are well-behaved.
2. If music, a painting or a play is *good*, it is enjoyable and well-done.
3. Someone who is caring and kind is *good*.

goodbye

'*Goodbye*' is what you say when you leave someone.

goodnight

'*Goodnight*' is what you say when you leave someone at night.

goods

Goods are things that can be bought and sold.

goose
(geese)

A *goose* is a large bird that swims, flies and lays eggs. *Geese* are bigger than ducks and have long beaks. They are very bad-tempered and are sometimes used to guard houses in the country.

grandfather
(grandfathers)

Your *grandfather* is the father of your mother or your father. Some people call their grandfather *grandpa* or *grandad*.

grandmother
(grandmothers)

Your *grandmother* is the mother of your mother or your father. Some people call their grandmother *grandma, nan* or *granny*.

a b c d e f **g** h i j k l m

grass

Grass is the plant that grows thickly in fields and on lawns and hillsides. It has thin green leaves. Cattle and other animals eat grass.

great
(greater, greatest)

Great is something very big, grand and wonderful.

greedy
(greedier, greediest)

Greedy people and animals eat more than they need.

groan
(groans, groaning, groaned)

If you *groan,* you make a low moaning sound because you are unhappy or in pain.

ground

The *ground* is the earth under your feet.

group
(groups)

A *group* is a number of people or things which are together in one place.

grow
(grows, growing, grew, grown)

If something *grows,* it gets bigger.

n o p q r s t u v w x y z

growl
(growls, growling, growled)

If a dog *growls*, it makes a deep, rumbling, angry sound.

guard
(guards, guarding, guarded)

1. A *guard* is a person who watches over people, places or objects to keep them safe.
2. If you *guard* something, you watch over it to keep it safe.

guess
(guesses, guessing, guessed)

If you make a *guess*, you give an answer to a question when you do not really know the answer.

guide
(guides, guiding, guided)

1. A *guide* gives you information about a place.

2. If you *guide* someone, you show them the way to go.

gun
(guns)

A *gun* is a weapon that shoots bullets.

guy
(guys)

You can call a group of friends '*guys*'. They can be boys or girls.

a b c d e f **g h** i j k l m

Hh

hair
(hair or hairs)

Hair grows on the heads and bodies of people and animals. It is made up of many fine threads. Someone or something that has a great deal of hair is called *hairy*.

hall
(halls)

The *hall* in a house is the part inside the front door that leads to other rooms.

hang
(hangs, hanging, hanged, hung)

If you *hang* something up, you put it on a hook so it does not touch the ground.

happen
(happens, happening, happened)

If something *happens*, it takes place.

n o p q r s t u v w x y z   73

hard
(harder, hardest)

1. If something is *hard*, it is not soft.
2. If something is *hard* to do, it is difficult.

hare
(hares)

A *hare* is an animal like a rabbit, but larger with long ears and long legs. It can move very fast.

hat
(hats)

A *hat* is a covering for your head when you go outside.

hatch
(hatches,
hatching,
hatched)

When something *hatches*, it comes out of an egg.

hate
(hates, hating,
hated)

If you *hate* something or someone, you do not like them at all.

a b c d e f g **h** i j k l m

head
(heads)

Your *head* is the part of your body that holds your brain, eyes, nose and mouth.

health

Your *health* is how your body feels. When you are well, you are *healthy*.

hear
(hears, hearing, heard)

When you *hear* things, you notice sounds through your ears.

heaven

Heaven is a place where happiness never ends. Many people believe that God lives there and that people who are good go to heaven when they die.

heavy
(heavier, heaviest)

Something *heavy* is difficult to lift or carry.

hedgehog
(hedgehogs)

A *hedgehog* is a small brown animal which is covered in prickles.

n o p q r s t u v w x y z

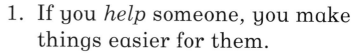

help
(helps, helping, helped)

1. If you *help* someone, you make things easier for them.

HELP!

2. If you call out 'Help!', you want to be heard because you are in danger and you want someone to rescue you.

hen
(hens)

A *hen* is a chicken that lays eggs.

herd
(herds, herding, herded)

1. A *herd* is a group of animals that are kept together. A *herdsman* looks after the herd as his job.

2. If you *herd* people or animals, you gather them together as a group.

hero
(heroes)

A *hero* is a boy or a man who has done something very brave. A girl or woman who does something very brave is called a *heroine*.

a b c d e f g **h** i j k l m

hide
(hides, hiding, hid, hidden)

If you *hide* from someone, you get into a place where no one can see you.

high
(higher, highest)

Something that is *high* goes up a long way.

hill
(hills)

A *hill* is ground which is higher than the ground around it.

hippopotamus
(hippopotamuses or hippopotami)

A *hippopotamus* is a large, heavy African animal that spends a great deal of time in rivers and lakes.

history

History is time in the past.

hit
(hits, hitting, hit)

If you *hit* something or someone, you strike them or knock them.

hole
(holes)

A *hole* is an opening in something.

home
(homes)

A *home* is a place to live.

honey

Honey is the sweet, yellow liquid that bees make. People often eat honey on bread.

hop
(hops, hopping, hopped)

If you *hop*, you jump about on one foot.

horse
(horses)

A *horse* is a large animal which people ride. Some *horses* are used for pulling coaches, carts or ploughs.

hospital
(hospitals)

A *hospital* is a place where people go to be cared for when they are sick or hurt.

a b c d e f g **h** i j k l m

hot
(hotter, hottest)

Something *hot* is very warm.

hour
(hours)

An *hour* is a length of time. An hour is 60 minutes. A day has 24 *hours*.

house
(houses)

A *house* is a building where people live together.

huge
(huger, hugest)

Something *huge* is very, very big.

hump
(humps)

A *hump* is a big lump, like the hump that a camel has on its back.

hungry
(hungrier,
hungriest)

If you are *hungry*, your stomach feels empty and you want something to eat.

n o p q r s t u v w x y z

hunt
(hunts, hunting, hunted)

1. When a group of people search for the same thing, they have a *hunt*. A *treasure hunt* is a party game when everyone looks for the prize.
2. When you *hunt* for something, you look carefully for it.
3. People who *hunt* wild animals go after them to trap or kill them. These people are called *hunters* or *huntsmen* if they are on horseback. They often use dogs for *hunting*.

hurry
(hurries, hurrying, hurried)

If you *hurry*, you move very quickly so you will not be late.

hutch
(hutches)

A *hutch* is a home for a rabbit.

a b c d e f g **h** **i** j k l m

ice

Ice is water that has frozen hard.

ice-cream
(ice-creams)

Ice-cream is a sweet, frozen food that tastes creamy. There are many different flavours of ice-cream, like strawberry, chocolate and toffee.

idea
(ideas)

An *idea* is something that you have thought of yourself.

ill

If you are *ill*, there is something wrong with you. You may have an *illness*, like measles or 'flu.

inch
(inches)

An *inch* is a measurement of length.

incredible

If something is *incredible*, it is difficult to believe.

n o p q r s t u v w x y z

index
(indexes)

An *index* is a list at the back of a book. It is in alphabetical order and tells you where to find things in the book.

information

Information is a collection of words that tell you about something or someone.

initial
(initials)

Initials are the first letters of words. For example, GL are the initials of this dictionary writer.

interesting

Interesting things make you want to find out more about them.

introduction
(introductions)

The *introduction* to something is at the beginning. In a book, the introduction tells you about the book and what is in it.

invitation
(invitations)

Invitation

Dear Rashid

Please come to my Birthday Party at 3pm on March 13th at:

316 Harcourt Street Broomhill Glasgow G11 5PD

Love from Shirley

An *invitation* asks you to come to something, like a party.

a b c d e f g h i j k l m

jacket
(jackets)

A *jacket* is a piece of clothing which is like a short coat.

jam
(jams)

Jam is made from fruit boiled with sugar until it is thick. Jam is spread on bread or cakes.

jeans

Jeans are trousers made from a thick, hard-wearing cloth.

job
(jobs)

1. A *job* is work that someone does for money.
2. A *job* is something that has to be done.

join
(joins, joining, joined)

1. When you *join* something, you put the two parts together to make one thing.
2. If you *join* a group or a club, you become part of it.

n o p q r s t u v w x y z

juice
(juice or juices)

Juice is the liquid that comes out of fruit when you squeeze it.

jumble sale
(jumble sales)

A *jumble sale* is a sale to raise money for charity. People give all the things they don't want any more and other people buy them for small amounts of money.

jump
(jumps, jumping, jumped)

When you *jump,* you move up and down suddenly into the air.

a b c d e f g h i j k l m

Kk

keep
(keeps, keeping, kept)

1. If you *keep* something, you have it for yourself.
2. If you are told to '*Keep off*' or to '*Keep away*' from something, you must not go near it.

kick
(kicks, kicking, kicked)

If you *kick* something, like a ball, you hit it hard with your foot.

kill
(kills, killing, killed)

If a person *kills* an animal or a person, they make them die.

king
(kings)

A *king* is the man who rules a country.

kitchen
(kitchens)

A *kitchen* is a room in a house where food is prepared and cooked. The washing-up is also done in the kitchen.

kitten
(kittens)

A *kitten* is a baby cat.

knee
(knees)

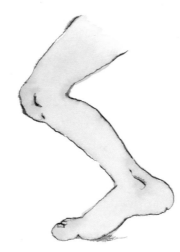

Your *knee* is the joint in your leg. It is the place where your leg bends.

knit
(knits, knitting, knitted)

When you *knit*, you use wool and a pair of needles to make clothes like jumpers.

know
(knows, knowing, knew, known)

If you *know* something, you have something in your mind that you have found out or learnt. If many people know the same information, it is *well-known*.

a b c d e f g h i j **k l** m

ladder
(ladders)

A *ladder* is made of two long poles with short bars between them so that you can climb up and down.

lady
(ladies)

Lady is a polite name for a woman.

lake
(lakes)

A *lake* is an area of fresh water with land all around it.

lamb
(lambs)

A *lamb* is a baby sheep.

land
(lands, landing, landed)

1. *Land* is the part of the world that is not covered by sea. It is dry ground.
2. If a boat or an aeroplane *lands*, it arrives.

large
(larger, largest)

Something *large* is big.

laugh
(laughs,
laughing,
laughed)

If you *laugh*, you make the sound that people make when they are happy or think something is funny.

lead
(leads, leading,
led)

If you *lead* someone to a place, you take them there to show them the way.

leaf
(leaves)

A *leaf* is one of the thin, flat parts of a plant. Leaves are usually green.

leap
(leaps, leaping,
leapt)

If you *leap*, you jump a long way.

learn
(learns, learning,
learned or learnt)

When you *learn* about something, you find out about it or how to do it.

a b c d e f g h i j k l m

leave
(leaves, leaving, left)

If you *leave* something, you do not take it with you.

left

1. Your *left* hand is the opposite to your right hand.
2. See leave

leg
(legs)

Your *legs* are the two long parts of your body that you use for walking.

lemonade

Lemonade is a drink made from the juice of lemons. It is usually fizzy and sweet.

letter
(letters)

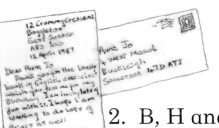

1. A *letter* is a message that someone writes to you and sends through the post.
2. B, H and V are *letters*. There are 26 letters in the alphabet.

level
(levels)

1. If something is *level,* it is flat.
2. The *level* of a liquid in a container, or the level of a lake or river, is how high up it is.

lick
(licks, licking, licked)

If you *lick* something, you move your tongue across it to taste it, to make it wet or to clean it.

lid
(lids)

A *lid* is the top of a box or container which can be taken off.

lie
(lies, lying, lay, lain)

If you *lie* somewhere, you rest your body flat on something.

life
(lives)

Life is being alive. Humans, plants and animals all have life.

lift
(lifts, lifting, lifted)

If you *lift* something, you move it upwards to a higher place.

light
(lights)

1. *Light* is the brightness that lets you see. Light comes from the sun, the moon, candles, fire and lamps.
2. A *light* is anything that gives you brightness in the dark and lets you see.

lighthouse
(lighthouses)

A *lighthouse* is a tower built near the coast or on small islands in the sea. It has a strong flashing light at the top. The light flashes to guide ships or to warn them of danger.

lightning

Lightning is a very bright and sudden flash of light in the sky which happens during a thunderstorm.

lion
(lions)

A *lion* is a large animal of the cat family which lives in Africa and Southern Asia. A female lion is called a *lioness*.

list
(lists)

A *list* is a set of things that you write down one below the other.

litter

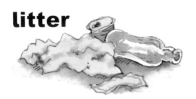

Litter is rubbish, such as waste paper and empty bottles, that is left lying around.

little
(littler, littlest)

If something is *little*, it is very small.

n o p q r s t u v w x y z   91

live
(lives, living,
lived)

If something *lives*, it is alive.

living

see live

lizard
(lizards)

A *lizard* is a small creature with
four short legs and a long tail.
Lizards are reptiles and have rough,
dry skins.

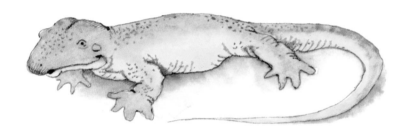

load
(loads, loading,
loaded)

If someone *loads* a vehicle, they put
things in it, usually to take them
somewhere else.

local

Local means belonging to a place
nearby. The local shops are the
shops near to where you are.

lolly
(lollies)

A *lolly* is a sweet or a flavoured ice
on a stick.

a b c d e f g h i j k l m

lonely
(lonelier,
loneliest)

If you are *lonely*, you feel unhappy because you have no friends.

long
(longer, longest)

1. If something takes a *long* time, it takes a lot of time.
2. If a road is *long*, it is a great distance from one end to the other.

look
(looks, looking, looked)

If you *look* at something, you use your eyes to see what is there.

loop
(loops)

A *loop* is a curved shape in something like wire, thread or ribbon.

lorry
(lorries)

A *lorry* is a large machine on wheels that carries heavy loads for long distances.

lose
(loses, losing, lost)

1. If you *lose* something, you cannot find it.
2. If you are *lost,* you do not know where you are or cannot find the people you were with.

loud
(louder, loudest)

Something *loud* makes a lot of noise and is easy to hear.

love
(loves, loving, loved)

1. *Love* is a very strong feeling you have when you like someone very much.
2. If you *love* someone or something, you like them very much.

lovely
(lovelier, loveliest)

Something *lovely* is beautiful to look at or listen to.

low
(lower, lowest)

Something that is *low* is close to the ground.

a b c d e f g h i j k l m

lower
(lowers, lowering, lowered)

If you *lower* something, you slowly move it downwards.

luck
(luckier, luckiest)

Luck is something good that happens without any reason to explain it. If you are *lucky*, you have good luck.

lump
(lumps)

A *lump* is a piece of something solid like a lump of wood, or a sugar lump. If something like custard is *lumpy*, it is not smooth and has bits in it.

lunch
(lunches)

Lunch is the meal that you have in the middle of the day.

lying

see lie

machine
(machines)

A *machine* is something with several parts that work together to do a job. *Machines* usually work by electricity or have an engine. Cars, computers and cookers are all machines.

machinery

Machinery means a collection of machines.

magic

Magic is the power to do wonderful things or tricks that are usually impossible to do.

mail

Mail is another name for letters and parcels that the postman brings.

a b c d e f g h i j k l **m**

make
(makes, making, made)

1. When you *make* something, you shape it or build it by putting things together.
2. If you *make way* for someone, you move out of their way to let them go past.

male
(males)

Any person or animal who can be a father is *male*.

man
(men)

A *man* is a grown-up boy.

map
(maps)

A *map* is a drawing of a place as it would look from above. It shows the shape of the land, the mountains and rivers, the towns, villages and cities, the roads and railways.

market
(markets)

A *market* is a place, usually in the open air, where things are bought and sold at stalls.

materials   *Materials* are the things you need to make something.

may
1. When you say that something *may* be true, you mean it could be true but you are not sure.
2. If you say '*May* I have one?', you are asking politely for something.

mean
(means,
meaning, meant;
meaner,
meanest)
1. If you ask someone what they *mean*, you want something explained to you.
2. If a person is *mean*, they are unkind and unpleasant.

meat
(meats)

Meat is the flesh of animals that we eat.

medical   *Medical* means things to do with people's health.

meet
(meets, meeting, met)
When people *meet*, they come to a place together and say 'hello'.

men   see man

a b c d e f g h i j k l **m**

mend
(mends,
mending,
mended)

If you *mend* something, you put it back together after it has been broken.

mess

If things are in a *mess*, they are untidy. People who leave things lying around, or who spill things, are *messy*.

message
(messages)

A *message* is words or information that you leave for someone when you cannot speak to them.

met

see meet

metre
(metres)

A *metre* is a measurement of length.

mice

see mouse

n o p q r s t u v w x y z

middle

The *middle* of something is halfway between the beginning and the end, or halfway between the top and the bottom.

mighty
(mightier,
mightiest)

If a person is *mighty*, they are very strong.

mile
(miles)

A *mile* is a measurement of distance. It is equal to 1·6 kilometres.

milk

Milk is a white liquid that comes from cows and goats. People can drink milk.

mill
(mills)

A *mill* is a building where grain is crushed to make flour.

mind
(minds, minding,
minded)

1. If you *mind* about something, you care about it.
2. If you *change your mind*, you do not do what you were going to do in the first place.

a b c d e f g h i j k l **m**

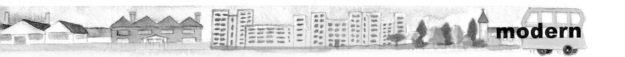
mine
(mines)

A *mine* is a place underground where people work to dig out coal, jewels, salt or metals.

minute
(minutes)

One *minute* is a measure of time. It is 60 seconds. There are 60 *minutes* in one hour.

mirror
(mirrors)

A *mirror* is a flat piece of glass in which you can see yourself.

Miss

Miss is the polite way of writing or speaking to a woman who is not married. You say *Miss Jones* or *Miss Hayes*.

missing

If someone is *missing*, he or she is not where they should be.

modern

Modern means the kind of things that are to do with life around you now.

mole
(moles)

A *mole* is a small animal that lives underground. It has tiny eyes and short dark fur.

money

Money is the coins and pieces of paper used when people buy and sell things.

monster
(monsters)

A *monster* is a huge, terrifying creature that you find in stories.

moon
(moons)

The *moon* is a planet. It goes round our planet once in every four weeks. The moon shines at night.

morning
(mornings)

Morning is the first part of the day; from sunrise until lunchtime.

a b c d e f g h i j k l **m**

moth
(moths)

A *moth* is an insect with wings. *Moths* usually fly at night.

mother
(mothers)

A *mother* is a woman with a child or children of her own.

motor
(motors)

A *motor* is the part inside a machine that makes it work.

mount
(mounts,
mounting,
mounted)

If you *mount* something, like a horse, you get on its back.

mountain
(mountains)

A *mountain* is a very high hill. It is often steep and difficult to climb.

mouse
(mice)

A *mouse* is a tiny animal with sharp teeth, whiskers and a long tail.

mouth
(mouths)

Your *mouth* is the opening in your face that you use for eating and speaking.

move
(moves, moving, moved)

1. When you *move*, you go from one place to another.
2. When you *move* something, you take it from one place and put it in another.

movement
(movements)

If you see or hear a *movement*, you notice someone or something moving.

mud

Mud is a wet and sticky mixture of earth and water. If you walk or play in mud, you get *muddy*.

mum
(mums)

Mum or *mummy* is a family name for mother.

music

Music is made up of sounds that people sing or play on instruments.

mystery
(mysteries)

A *mystery* is something strange and puzzling that has happened.

a b c d e f g h i j k l **m**

name
(names)

Your *name* is what you are called.

neighbour
(neighbours)

Your *neighbours* are the people who live near you.

nest
(nests)

A *nest* is a warm home for a bird or a small animal.

net
(nets)

Fishermen use a *net* to catch fish.

new
(newer, newest)

1. *New* things have just been bought or made.
2. *New* things are different.

news

News is information about things that have just happened.

night
(nights)

Night is the time between sunset and sunrise when it is dark and most people, and many animals, are asleep.

noise
(noises)

A *noise* is a sound. It is often loud.

nomad
(nomads)

A *nomad* is one of a group of people who move from place to place.

north

North is one of the four main compass points.

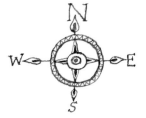

nose
(noses)

You breathe and smell with your *nose*.

nurse
(nurses)

A *nurse* is a person whose job is to look after you if you are hurt or ill and in hospital.

a b c d e f g h i j k l m

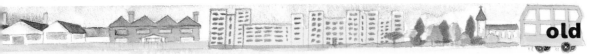

oasis
(oases)

An *oasis* is a place in the desert where there is water and where plants or trees grow.

oil
(oils)

1. *Oil* is a thick, smooth liquid that is found underground. It is used to keep engines running smoothly.
2. Some *oil* is made from plants and can be used for cooking or for making dressings.
3. Some *oils* are used to rub onto your skin to protect you from the sun or to make your skin soft.

old
(older, oldest)

1. A person or animal that is *old* has lived for a long time.
2. Something that is *old* has been around for a long time.

n o p q r s t u v w x y z

107

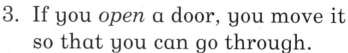

open
(opens, opening, opened)

1. If something is *open*, it is not shut.
2. If you *open* something like a box, you take off the lid.
3. If you *open* a door, you move it so that you can go through.
4. If something like a seed *opens*, it breaks apart.

orange
(oranges)

An *orange* is a round, juicy fruit.

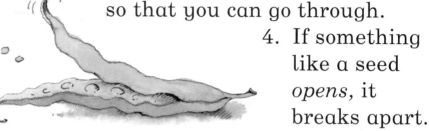

order
(orders, ordering, ordered)

1. If you *order* something from a shop, you ask them to get it for you.
2. If a shopkeeper has an *order*, he or she has to get something for a customer.

ordinary

Ordinary things are not unusual. You can see ordinary things all the time.

a b c d e f g h i j k l m

otter
(otters)

An *otter* is a rare animal that lives near water. It has short brown fur, a long tail and webbed feet. *Otters* can swim and live on fish and other small animals.

out

1. *Out* is not in.
2. If a fire is *out*, it is not burning any more.

outside
(outsides)

1. The *outside* of something is the surface or the edges of it.
2. If you are *outside*, you are in the open air.

n o p q r s t u v w x y z

pack
(packs, packing,
packed)

1. A *pack* is a group of something,
like a *pack of cubs* or a *pack of
dogs*.

2. If you *pack* things, you put them
together in a box or in a bundle.

packet
(packets)

A *packet* is a small parcel.

page
(pages)

A *page* is one side
of paper in a book
or on a pad.

110

a b c d e f g h i j k l m

paint
(paints, painted, painting)

1. *Paint* is a coloured liquid that is put on a surface with a brush or a roller.
2. If you *paint* something, you use a brush, roller or your hands to put coloured liquid on it.

pair
(pairs)

A *pair* is two things that belong together, like a *pair of scissors* or a *pair of shoes*.

paper
(papers)

1. *Paper* is the material that you write on, wrap things with, and paint on.
2. A *paper* is another name for a newspaper.

parent
(parents)

A *parent* is a mother or a father.

park
(parks)

A *park* is an open space in a town where people can go to walk, sit or play and enjoy themselves.

party
(parties)

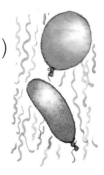

When you have a *party*, you ask your friends to come and share a special occasion with you.

pass
(passes, passing, passed)

1. When you *pass* someone or something, you go by.
2. If you *pass* a ball to another player in a game, you give it to them.

passenger
(passengers)

A *passenger* is anyone who travels in a car, boat, aeroplane or on a train. The driver is not a passenger.

past

The *past* is time gone by.

path
(paths)

A *path* is a narrow way through somewhere.

a b c d e f g h i j k l m

patrol
(patrols,
patrolling,
patrolled)

1. A *patrol* is a group of people, like the police or soldiers, who walk around an area to see what is going on there.
2. When a group of people, like the police, *patrol* an area, they walk around it to see that there is no danger.

pattern
(patterns)

A *pattern* is lines or shapes that have been drawn over and over again.

paw
(paws)

A *paw* is the foot of an animal. It has soft pads underneath and claws on each toe.

pea
(peas)

A *pea* is a small round seed which grows in a pod. *Peas* are eaten as vegetables.

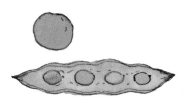

peace

Peace is a feeling of quiet and calm. If the day is *peaceful*, it is quiet.

people   Men, women and children are all *people*.

perch
(perches)   A *perch* is a seat for a bird.

perform
(performs,
performing,
performed)

When you *perform*, you do something, like a dance, in front of a group of people.

person
(persons or
people)   A *person* is a man, a woman or a child.

pest
(pests)   A *pest* is any person or animal that causes a great deal of trouble.

pet
(pets)   A *pet* is an animal that you like and keep in your home.

a b c d e f g h i j k l m

petrol

Petrol is a liquid made from oil. You use petrol as a fuel for motors. Petrol makes cars move.

pick
(picks, picking, picked)

1. If you *pick* one thing from several, you choose it.
2. If you *pick* fruit or flowers, you break them off and take them.

picture
(pictures)

A *picture* is a drawing, painting or photograph.

piece
(pieces)

A *piece* of something is a bit of it.

pig
(pigs)

A *pig* is a farm animal. It has thick skin and a curly tail.

pipe
(pipes)

1. A *pipe* is a long hollow tube that can be used to bring water, oil or other liquids from one place to another.
2. A *pipe* is a small tube with a bowl at the end that some people use for smoking tobacco.

pirate
(pirates)

A *pirate* is a robber who steals from ships at sea.

pit
(pits)

1. A *pit* is a large hole in the ground.
2. A *pit* is a coal mine. The opening to a pit is called the *pithead*.

pizza
(pizzas)

A *pizza* is a flat, round piece of dough which is covered with tomatoes, cheese and other things and then baked in a very hot oven.

a b c d e f g h i j k l m

place
(places)

A *place* is a particular area or building.

plant
(plant, planting, planted)

1. A *plant* is a living thing that grows in the ground.
2. If you *plant* something, you put the seed, bulb or root into the ground so that it will grow.

plate
(plates)

A *plate* is a flat, round dish for serving and eating food.

play
(plays, playing, played)

1. When you *play*, you are in a game.
2. A *play* is a story that you act out. Sometimes you can use puppets.

playground
(playgrounds)

A *playground* is a piece of land especially for children to play in.

pleasant
(pleasanter,
pleasantest)

Something that is *pleasant* is nice to listen to or to look at.

please
(pleases,
pleasing,
pleased)

1. If you *please* someone, you make them happy.
2. If you say *'please'*, you are asking for something politely.

plough
(ploughs,
ploughing,
ploughed)

1. A *plough* is a farm machine that the farmer uses to turn over the earth before he plants the seeds for crops.
2. If the farmer *ploughs* a field, he uses a machine to break up the earth.

pocket
(pockets)

A *pocket* is like a bag sewn into your clothes. You use a pocket to carry small things like money or a handkerchief.

118   a b c d e f g h i j k l m

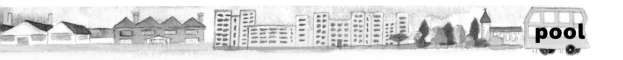

police

The *police* are the men and women who work to keep the laws of the country.

polish
(polishes,
polishing,
polished)

1. You use *polish* to make things shine. There are different kinds of polish, like *nail polish* or *furniture polish*.
2. When you *polish* something, you rub it with a cloth to make it shine.

pond
(ponds)

A *pond* is a small lake.

pony
(ponies)

A *pony* is a small horse.

pool
(pools)

A *pool* is a small piece of quiet water.

poor
(poorer, poorest)

People who are *poor* do not have much money.

post
(posts, posting, posted)

1. The *post* is the letters and parcels that the *postman* or *postwoman* delivers to your house.

2. If you *post* a letter or parcel, you send it to someone by post. You must use the correct address and the *postcode* to show exactly where it must be delivered to. You put the letter in a *post-box*.

potato
(potatoes)

A *potato* is a vegetable that grows under the ground. You cook it by boiling, frying or baking.

pour
(pours, pouring, poured)

1. If you *pour* a liquid, you tip it out of a container.

2. If the rain *pours*, it falls very heavily.

a b c d e f g h i j k l m

practice
(practices)

If you have a *practice*, like a cricket practice or a guitar practice, you do something over and over again to get better at it.

practise
(practises,
practising,
practised)

If you *practise* something, you do it over and over again to get better at it.

pray
(prays, praying,
prayed)

If you *pray*, you talk to God by saying a *prayer*.

present
(presents)

A *present* is something you are given to celebrate a special occasion, like a birthday.

pretty
(prettier,
prettiest)

Pretty things or people are pleasing to look at.

prey

The *prey* of an animal or bird is the creatures that it hunts for food.

price
(prices)

The *price* of something is how much money you must give to buy it.

prince
(princes)

A *prince* is the son of a king or queen.

princess
(princesses)

A *princess* is the daughter of a king or queen.

print
(prints, printing, printed)

1. When someone *prints* a poster, a newspaper or a book, they use a machine to copy the writing and pictures so that they can make lots of copies.

2. If someone *prints* a pattern or a picture on a tee-shirt, they use a machine to put the picture on it.

a b c d e f g h i j k l m

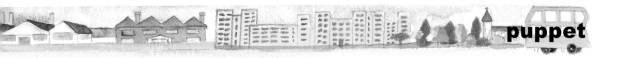

prize
(prizes)

A *prize* is something that you are given as a reward for being very good at something.

proud
(prouder,
proudest)

If you are *proud,* you are very pleased because you have done something very well.

public

If something is *public*, it is meant for everyone to use.

puddle
(puddles)

A *puddle* is a very small pool of water.

pull
(pulls, pulling,
pulled)

When you *pull* something, you get hold of it and make it come towards you.

puppet
(puppets)

A *puppet* is a kind of doll that you can move by using strings, rods or your hands.

puppy
(puppies)

A *puppy* is a baby dog.

pure
(purer, purest)

Something *pure* is clean and has nothing mixed with it.

push
(pushes,
pushing, pushed)

You *push* something when you press hard against it.

pyjamas

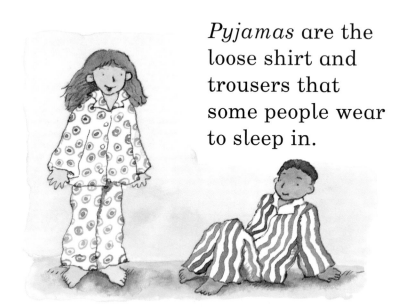

Pyjamas are the loose shirt and trousers that some people wear to sleep in.

a b c d e f g h i j k l m

quack
(quacks,
quacking,
quacked)

1. A *quack* is the sound that ducks make.
2. When a duck makes a sound, it *quacks*.

queen
(queens)

A *queen* is the female ruler of a country.

quick
(quicker,
quickest)

If you are *quick*, you can move very fast.

quiet
(quieter, quietest)

If you are *quiet*, you do not make much sound.

rabbit
(rabbits)

A *rabbit* is a small furry animal with long ears and a small white tail. *Rabbits* can hop very fast on their strong back legs. They live in tunnels called burrows. All the burrows together are called a warren.

race
(races, racing, raced)

1. A *race* is a competition to see who is the fastest.
2. If you *race,* you go as fast as you can to try to be the fastest.

rag
(rags)

A *rag* is an old piece of material.

railway
(railways)

A *railway* is a way of carrying people or things from one place to another by train. Trains run on *rails* which are fixed to a track.

a b c d e f g h i j k l m

rain
(rains, raining, rained)

1. *Rain* is the water that falls from the sky.
2. When it *rains*, little drops of water fall from the sky.

ran

see run

rang

see ring

rat
(rats)

A *rat* is a small animal with long sharp teeth. It has a long tail and looks like a large mouse.

raucous

Raucous sounds are unpleasant and very loud.

reach
(reaches, reaching, reached)

If you *reach* a place, you get there.

read
(reads, reading, read)

When you *read* something, you see and understand words that are written down.

remember
(remembers, remembering, remembered)

When you *remember* something, you keep it in your mind.

rescue
(rescues, rescuing, rescued)

If a person *rescues* someone, they save them from danger.

rest
(rests, resting, rested)

1. When you *rest*, you are still and relaxed.
2. If you have a *rest*, you stop what you have been doing for a while.
3. The *rest* means everything that is left.

restaurant
(restaurants)

A *restaurant* is a place where people go and pay money to have a meal.

a b c d e f g h i j k l m

rich
(richer, richest)

If you are *rich*, you have a lot of money.

ride
(rides, riding, rode, ridden)

1. If you *ride* a horse or a bicycle, you are on it while it is moving along.
2. A *ride* is a journey on a horse, a bicycle, in a car or a bus.

right

1. *Right* is correct or true.
2. *Right* is the opposite of left.

ring
(rings, ringing, rang, rung)

1. A *ring* is a circle.
2. If you *ring* a bell, you make it sound.
3. A *showjumping ring* is where horse riders have a competition.

ripe
(riper, ripest)

If fruit is *ripe*, it is ready to be eaten.

river
(rivers)

A *river* is a large amount of fresh water that flows from high land to the sea.

road
(roads)

A *road* is a long, hard piece of ground that takes traffic from one place to another.

roar
(roars, roaring, roared)

A *roar* is a loud, deep sound, like the sound of a lion or of thunder.

robin
(robins)

A *robin* is a bird with a red breast. You usually see *robins* during the winter.

rock
(rocks)

A *rock* is a large piece of stone.

rode

see ride

rodeo
(rodeos)

A *rodeo* is a competition where cowboys try to stay on the back of a wild horse or bull.

roll
(rolls, rolling, rolled)

If you *roll*, you turn over and over. A machine that has a huge wheel on the front is called a *roller*.

a b c d e f g h i j k l m

parse

roof
(roofs)

A *roof* is the covering on top of a house or any other building.

room
(rooms)

A *room* is one of the spaces inside a building that has its own walls, ceiling and floor. The kitchen, the dining-room and the bedroom are all *rooms*.

root
(roots)

The *root* of a plant is the part that grows underground.

rope
(ropes)

Rope is made from very thick, strong pieces of string or wire which have been twisted together.

rose
(roses)

A *rose* is a flower with a pleasant smell. Most *roses* have thorns on their stems.

rough
(rougher, roughest)

If something is *rough*, it is bumpy or lumpy.

round
(rounder, roundest)

Something *round* is shaped like a circle or a ball.

roundabout
(roundabouts)

A *roundabout* is a machine with seats on it. You can ride on *roundabouts* in parks and at fairgrounds.

royal

Royal means to do with the king and queen.

rubbish

Rubbish is things that you throw away.

run
(runs, running, ran, run)

If you *run*, you use your legs to move very quickly.

rush
(rushes, rushing, rushed)

1. A *rush* of air, or water, is the sound of it moving very quickly and suddenly.
2. When you *rush*, you hurry.

rustle
(rustles, rustling, rustled)

If you hear a *rustle*, the sound you hear is like the soft moving of dry leaves when the wind blows through them. If you hear something *rustling*, it might be an animal moving quietly in the bushes.

a b c d e f g h i j k l m

sack
(sacks)

A *sack* is a large bag made of cloth or plastic.

sad
(sadder, saddest)

If you are *sad*, you are unhappy about something.

saddle
(saddles)

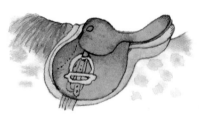

A *saddle* is a seat for an animal's back or a bicycle, so that you can ride on it comfortably.

safari
(safaris)

A *safari* is a journey that a group of people make to watch or hunt wild animals.

safe
(safer, safest)

If you are *safe*, you are away from danger. If you do something *safely*, you make sure you cannot be harmed while you are doing it.

sail
(sails, sailing, sailed)

1. A *sail* is a large piece of material fixed to the mast of a ship or boat. When the sail fills with wind it makes the ship or boat move along.
2. If a boat *sails*, it moves across the water using the wind for power.

sand

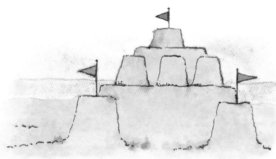

Sand is very tiny grains of rock that you find on beaches or in the desert. You can build a *sand castle* with sand.

sandwich
(sandwiches)

A *sandwich* is two pieces of bread with a filling of food in between them.

saucepan
(saucepans)

A *saucepan* is a metal pot with a handle, which is used for cooking. It often has a lid.

sausage
(sausages)

A *sausage* is made from very tiny pieces of meat mixed with other things like bread or herbs. You can grill or fry a sausage before you eat it.

a b c d e f g h i j k l m

save
(saves, saving, saved)

If you *save* someone, you get them out of danger.

scarecrow
(scarecrows)

A farmer uses a *scarecrow* to frighten birds away from the crops in the fields. A scarecrow usually looks like a person because it is dressed in old clothes.

scarf
(scarves)

A *scarf* is a long piece of material that you wear around your neck to keep warm.

school
(schools)

A *school* is a place where young people go to learn.

scissors

Scissors are tools for cutting. They have two blades that are joined together.

scratch
(scratches, scratching, scratched)

If something *scratches* you, it scrapes your skin and feels sharp. You may have a small cut.

screech
(screeches,
screeching,
screeched)

If you *screech*, you make an unpleasant, loud, high-sounding noise.

sea
(seas)

A *sea* is a very large area of salt water.

seal
(seals)

A *seal* is a large animal that eats fish and lives partly on land and partly in the sea.

search
(searches,
searching,
searched)

When you *search* for something, you look very hard for it.

seat
(seats)

A *seat* is something to sit on.

second
(seconds)

A *second* is a measurement of time. There are 60 *seconds* in one minute.

a b c d e f g h i j k l m

see
(sees, seeing, saw, seen)

If you *see* something, you use your eyes to look at something.

seed
(seeds)

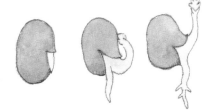

A *seed* is the small, hard part of a plant that grows into a new plant when you put it into the ground.

sell
(sells, selling, sold)

When you *sell* something, you let someone have it in return for money.

send
(sends, sending, sent)

If you *send* something, you make it go somewhere.

sense
(senses)

Your *senses* are your powers to see, feel, smell, taste and hear.

several

If you have *several* things, you have more than two, but not many more.

shake
(shakes, shaking, shook, shaken)

If you *shake* something, you move it quickly up and down or from side to side.

shape
(shapes)

The *shape* of something is the way its outside edges look. The shape of a ball is round; a box is square.

circle   *triangle*   *square*

share
(shares, sharing, shared)

When you *share* something, you give some of what you have to someone else.

sharp
(sharper, sharpest)

Something *sharp* has an edge or blades that can cut.

shed
(sheds)

A *shed* is a small building that is used for storing things like garden tools.

    a b c d e f g h i j k l m

sheep
(sheep)

A *sheep* is a farm animal with a thick, woolly coat. Sheep are usually kept for their wool or their meat. A *sheepdog* looks after the sheep with the farmer.

shelf
(shelves)

A *shelf* is a flat piece of wood, metal or glass that is fixed to a wall or put inside a cupboard. You can keep all kinds of things on a shelf.

shell
(shells)

A *shell* is the thin, hard part round an egg, nut or some small animals, like snails.

shepherd
(shepherds)

A *shepherd* is a person whose job is to look after sheep.

sheriff
(sheriffs)

A *sheriff* is a person in America who is chosen to make sure that people obey the law.

shine
(shines, shining, shone)

When something *shines*, it gives out bright light.

shirt
(shirts)

A *shirt* is a piece of clothing for the top half of the body.

shoe
(shoes)

Shoes are things that you wear on your feet to keep them warm and dry. Some shoes have *shoelaces* to do them up.

shoot
(shoots, shooting, shot)

If you *shoot*, you use a gun or a bow and arrow to fire at a target.

shop
(shops, shopping, shopped)

1. A *shop* is a place where you can buy things. It is looked after by a *shopkeeper*.
2. When you buy things in a shop, you are *shopping*.

a b c d e f g h i j k l m

short
(shorter, shortest)

1. If something takes a *short* time, it happens quickly.
2. If something is a *short* distance away, it is not far from where you are.

shout
(shouts, shouting, shouted)

1. A *shout* is a short, loud cry.
2. If you *shout*, you call out very loudly.

show
(shows, showing, showed)

1. A *show* is an arrangement of things for people to look at.

2. If you *show* someone something, you let them look at it.

shower
(showers)

1. A *shower* is a short, light fall of rain.
2. A *shower* is usually in a bathroom. You stand under a spray of water so that you can wash.

shut
(shuts, shutting, shut)

If you *shut* something like a door, you close it.

shy
(shyer, shyest)

A *shy* person is afraid to meet people that they do not know.

side
(sides)

The *side* of something is the part to the left or right of the front and the back.

sigh
(sighs, sighing, sighed)

If you *sigh*, you breathe out slowly and heavily so that other people can hear you.

sign
(signs)

A *sign* is a piece of wood or metal that tells you things without speaking words.

silly
(sillier, silliest)

If you are *silly*, you are not clever.

silver

Silver is a precious metal that is made into jewellery and ornaments.

sing
(sings, singing, sang, sung)

When you *sing*, you make music with your voice.

a b c d e f g h i j k l m

sister
(sisters)

Your *sister* is a girl who has the same parents as you.

site
(sites)

A building *site* is a place where building is going on.

size
(sizes)

The *size* of something is how big or small it is.

skateboard
(skateboards)

A *skateboard* is a small board on wheels that you stand on while it moves along.

skill
(skills)

Skill is being able to do something well. If you have musical *skills*, you are good at music.

skin
(skins)

Skin covers the bodies of humans, animals and insects.

skip
(skips, skipping,
skipped)

When you *skip*,
you hop on one
leg and then the
other, as if you
are dancing.

skirt
(skirts)

A *skirt* is a piece of clothing for girls
and women to wear. *Skirts* hang
from the waist.

sky
(skies)

The *sky* is the space above the
earth. The sun, moon and stars are
in the sky.

sleep
(sleeps, sleeping,
slept)

When you *sleep*, you rest with your
eyes shut and you do not know
what is happening around you.

sleeve
(sleeves)

A *sleeve* is the part of a coat, shirt
or dress that covers the arm.

slip
(slips, slipping,
slipped)

If you *slip*, you slide and sometimes
fall down.

a b c d e f g h i j k l m

slow
(slower, slowest)

Things that are *slow* do not move quickly. When you move *slowly*, you take a lot of time to move.

slug
(slugs)

A *slug* is a small creature like a snail, but without a shell.

small
(smaller, smallest)

Someone or something that is *small* is little.

smart
(smarter, smartest)

If you are *smart* in the way you dress, you look neat and tidy.

smell
(smells, smelling, smelled or smelt)

1. If you *smell* something, you use your nose to find out about it.
2. If something *smells*, you notice it with your nose.

smile
(smiles, smiling, smiled)

When you *smile*, you make a wide shape with your lips to show you are happy.

smooth
(smoother,
smoothest)

If something is *smooth*, it is flat with no bumps in it.

snack
(snacks)

A *snack* is a small, quick meal.

snake
(snakes)

A *snake* is a reptile without legs. Some *snakes* are poisonous.

snap
(snaps,
snapping,
snapped)

If a dog *snaps*, it shuts its mouth suddenly as if it is biting.

snow

Snow is small, thin, white flakes of frozen water. Snow falls from the sky when the weather is very cold.

soap
(soaps)

Soap is made from oil or fats. You use it to wash things. Sweet smells and colour are often added to make soap more pleasant to use.

a b c d e f g h i j k l m

sock
(socks)

A *sock* is a piece of clothing for your foot. *Socks* come in pairs.

soft
(softer, softest)

If something is *soft*, it is not hard.

sold

see sell

soldier
(soldiers)

A *soldier* is a person who works in an army.

sorry

'*Sorry*', is what you say when you have done something wrong and you want to make up for it.

sort
(sorts, sorting, sorted)

1. The *sort* of something is the kind or type it is. Chocolate drops and fruit gums are different *sorts* of sweets.
2. If you *sort* things, you put them in groups that are alike in some way.

sound
(sounds)

A *sound* is something that you can hear.

soup
(soups)

Soup is a liquid food made of meat or vegetables.

special

Special things are usually better or more important than anything else.

speckled

Speckled things are covered in small, coloured marks or spots.

speed
(speeds)

The *speed* of something is how fast or slowly it goes.

spider
(spiders)

A *spider* is a small creature with eight legs. Most *spiders* make webs to catch insects for food.

a b c d e f g h i j k l m

spin
(spins, spinning, spun)

1. When you *spin*, you make thread by twisting long, thin pieces of cotton or wool together very quickly.
2. When a spider or a butterfly *spins*, it makes a web or a cocoon.
3. If you *spin* something, you make it turn very quickly on a point.

spire
(spires)

A *spire* is the tall, pointed part on top of a church tower.

splash
(splashes, splashing, splashed)

If you *splash*, you make drops of liquid fly up in the air with a loud noise.

split
(splits, splitting, split)

1. If something *splits*, it cracks or tears.
2. If you do the *splits*, you sit on the floor with one leg straight out in front of you and the other straight out behind you.

sport
(sports)

Sports are games like football, netball and tennis.

spot
(spots, spotting, spotted)

1. A *spot* is a small mark on something.
2. A *spot* is a particular place, like a quiet spot in the garden.
3. If you *spot* something, you notice it.

spray
(sprays, spraying, sprayed)

If you *spray* water, you make it send out a lot of tiny drops of liquid.

squawk
(squawks, squawking, squawked)

If a bird *squawks*, it makes a sudden loud sound.

squeak
(squeaks, squeaking, squeaked)

If a person, an animal or a thing *squeaks*, it makes a tiny, high sound.

a b c d e f g h i j k l m

squeeze
(squeezes,
squeezing,
squeezed)

If you *squeeze* something, you press it between your hands.

squirrel
(squirrels)

A *squirrel* is a small furry animal with a long bushy tail. It eats things like nuts and seeds. A squirrel's nest is called a drey.

stair
(stairs)

Stairs are steps which go from one level to another. They are usually inside a building.

stall
(stalls)

A *stall* is a kind of small shop or table where things can be sold.

stand
(stands,
standing, stood)

When you *stand*, you are on your feet and your legs are straight.

star
(stars, starring, starred)

1. *Stars* are the tiny specks of bright light that you see in the sky at night.
2. If a person or an animal *stars* in a film or a play, they have the most important part in it.

stare
(stares, staring, stared)

If you *stare*, you look at someone or something without looking away.

start
(starts, starting, started)

1. The *start* of something is the beginning of it.
2. When something *starts*, it begins.

station
(stations)

A *station* is a building which is the headquarters of the Police or the Fire Service.

stay
(stays, staying, stayed)

If you *stay* somewhere, you go on being in the same place.

steal
(steals, stealing, stole, stolen)

If someone *steals* something, they take something that does not belong to them without asking.

a b c d e f g h i j k l m

stem
(stems)

The *stem* of a plant is the long, thin part in the middle. Leaves, fruit and flowers grow on a stem.

step
(steps, stepping, stepped)

If you *step*, you lift your foot and put it down in another place.

stick
(sticks, sticking, stuck)

1. A *stick* is a long, thin piece of wood.

2. If you *stick* two things together, you fix them together with glue. If something is *sticky*, it feels as if it has glue on it.
3. If you get *stuck* in a small place, you cannot move.

still
(stiller, stillest)

If you sit *still*, you do not move.

sting
(stings, stinging, stung)

If something *stings* you, it gives you a sharp little stab of pain.

stolen   see steal

stone   A *stone* is a
(stones)   small piece of rock.

stood   see stand

stop   If you *stop* what you are doing, you
(stops, stopping,   do not do it any more.
stopped)

store   1. A *store* is a shop.
(stores, storing,   2. If you *store* things, you put them
stored)   away for later.

story   A *story* can be written or spoken. A
(stories)   story tells you about something
that has happened. It can be true or
it can be made up.

straw   1. *Straw* is dry stalks of corn.
(straws)

2. A *straw* is a thin tube that you
use to drink through.

     a b c d e f g h i j k l m

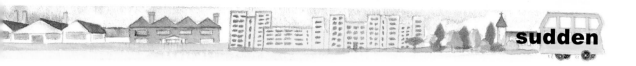

street
(streets)

A *street* is a road in a town with houses and a pavement.

stretch
(stretches,
stretching,
stretched)

When you *stretch*, you push your arms and legs away from your body. You often stretch when you are feeling tired.

stripe
(stripes)

A *stripe* is a coloured line across something.

strong
(stronger,
strongest)

People or animals that are *strong* are fit and healthy and able to carry heavy things.

stuck

see stick

sudden

If something is *sudden*, it happens quickly and without warning. It happens *suddenly*.

n o p q r **s** t u v w x y z   155

sugar

Sugar is powder or granules that you put in food to sweeten it.

suit
(suits)

A *suit* is a set of clothes with a top and bottom that match.

sun
(suns)

The *sun* is the brightest and closest star in the sky that gives the earth heat and light.

super

Super means extra special.

supermarket
(supermarkets)

A *supermarket* is a large shop where you can buy all sorts of food and things for the house.

supper
(suppers)

Supper is an early evening meal or snack that you have before you go to bed.

a b c d e f g h i j k l m

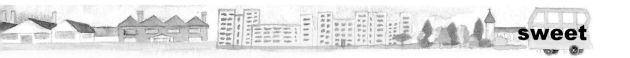

supply
(supplies,
supplying,
supplied)

1. If you have a *supply* of something, you have enough to use.
2. If you *supply* something, you give it to someone who wants it.

surface
(surfaces)

The *surface* of something is the outside or top part of it.

surprise
(surprises)

A *surprise* is something that happens when you are not expecting it.

surveyor
(surveyors)

A *surveyor* is a person whose job is to look at a piece of land or house very carefully before someone else buys it.

sweet
(sweets, sweeter,
sweetest)

1. A *sweet* is a small piece of food with lots of sugar in it.

2. *Sweet* food has sugar in it.

swim
(swims,
swimming, swam,
swum)

If you *swim*, you use your arms and legs to move yourself through water without touching the bottom. If you can swim, you are a *swimmer*.

swing
(swings,
swinging, swung)

1. A *swing* is a seat, which hangs from posts or from a tree, for people to play on.
2. If a monkey *swings* from tree to tree, it uses its arms to hold on to branches as it moves along.

symbol
(symbols)

A *symbol* is a shape or pattern that means something.

system
(systems)

A *system* is a set of parts that work together as one thing.

a b c d e f g h i j k l m

table
(tables)

A *table* is a piece of furniture with a flat top for putting things on.

tail
(tails)

A *tail* is the part of an animal, bird or fish that grows at the end of its body.

takeaway
(takeaways)

A *takeaway* is a cooked meal that you can buy in a shop or restaurant to eat somewhere else.

tale
(tales)

A *tale* is a story.

talk
(talks, talking, talked)

When you *talk*, you speak to other people.

tall
(taller, tallest)

Someone or something that is *tall* is very high.

taught

see teach

tea
(teas)

1. *Tea* is a drink made by pouring boiling water onto the dried leaves of the tea plant. You can have a drink of afternoon tea in a *teashop* at *teatime*.
2. *Tea* is a small meal in the afternoon or evening.

teacher
(teachers)

A *teacher* is a person whose job is to help people to learn.

team
(teams)

A *team* is a group of people who work or play a sport together.

a b c d e f g h i j k l m

teddy
(teddies)

A *teddy* is
a toy bear.

**tee shirt or
t-shirt**
(tee shirts or
t-shirts)

A *tee shirt* is
a top made
of soft,
comfortable
material.

teeth

see tooth

telephone
(telephones)

A *telephone* is a
machine that you use to
speak to people who are
in another place and
not with you.

television
(televisions)

A *television* is a machine that
brings pictures and sound through
the air by electricity. A *TV* is short
for a television.

tell
(tells, telling, told)

If you *tell* someone something, you pass on a story or information by speaking or writing to them.

terrible

If something is *terrible*, it is very, very bad.

thank
(thanks, thanking, thanked)

If you *thank* someone, you show them that you are pleased about something they have done for you.

thick
(thicker, thickest)

If you have *thick* hair, the strands grow closely together and you have a lot of it.

thief
(thieves)

A *thief* is a person who takes things that belong to someone else, without asking.

thing
(things)

A *thing* is anything that can be seen or touched. If you do not know what something is called, you say it is a 'thing'.

162   a b c d e f g h i j k l m

think
(thinks, thinking, thought)

When you *think*, you have words and ideas in your mind.

thirsty
(thirstier, thirstiest)

If you are *thirsty*, you need a drink.

thread
(threads)

A *thread* is a thin piece of something, like cotton, wool or nylon.

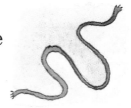

throat
(throats)

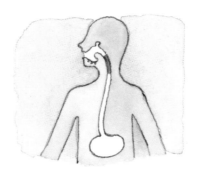

Your *throat* is the top of the tube that takes the food from your mouth into your stomach.

through

If you go *through* something, you go from one side to the other, or from one end to the other.

throw
(throws, throwing, threw, thrown)

When you *throw* something like a ball, you send it into the air with your hand.

n o p q r s **t** u v w x y z

thunder

Thunder is a loud noise in a storm. There is usually a loud rumble of thunder after lightning. Sometimes a *thunderbolt* strikes a tree or a high building.

tidy
(tidies, tidying, tidied)

If you *tidy*, you put things away in their proper place so that your room or house looks neat.

tie
(ties, tying, tied)

1. If you *tie* something, you fix it together with string or rope.
2. If you *tie* someone up, you put ropes around them to stop them getting away.

tiger
(tigers)

A *tiger* is a large, wild animal found in India and China. It has orange and black striped fur.

a b c d e f g h i j k l m

time

Time is what we measure in units of seconds, minutes, hours, days, weeks and so on.

tiny
(tinier, tiniest)

Something or someone that is *tiny* is very, very small.

tired

When you are *tired*, you want to rest or go to sleep.

toad
(toads)

A *toad* is an animal like a big frog. It has rough dry skin and lives in damp places on land.

toast

Toast is bread which has been cooked until it is brown and crisp.

today

Today is the day that it is now.

tomorrow

Tomorrow is the day after today.

tongue
(tongues)

Your *tongue* is the soft piece of flesh in your mouth that you can move. Your tongue helps you to taste, to eat and to speak.

tooth
(teeth)

A *tooth* is one of the hard, white objects that grow in your mouth. You use your *teeth* to bite and eat food. You use *toothpaste* to keep your teeth clean.

top
(tops)

The *top* of something is the highest part of it.

tortoise
(tortoises)

A *tortoise* is a small animal with a shell that covers its body. It moves very slowly.

a b c d e f g h i j k l m

touch
(touches,
touching,
touched)

If you *touch* something or someone, you feel them by putting your hand on them.

tower
(towers)

A *tower* is a very tall, narrow building.

town
(towns)

A *town* is a place with a lot of streets and buildings where people live and work.

toy
(toys)

A *toy* is something you play with.

track
(tracks, tracking, tracked)

1. A *track* is a special path where people and animals can practise running.
2. A *track* is a rough path through a wood or a farm.
3. If a dog *tracks* a missing object or person, it uses its nose to find them.

tractor
(tractors)

A *tractor* is a farm machine that can pull heavy weights. It has very large wheels at the back.

traffic

Traffic is all the cars, lorries, motorbikes, buses, bicycles and other things that travel on the road.

trail
(trails)

1. A *trail* is a rough path.
2. The *trail* of a snail is the silvery mark it leaves behind it when it slides along.

train
(trains)

A *train* has carriages, which are joined together, and is pulled by an engine. *Trains* travel along railway tracks.

travel
(travels,
travelling,
travelled)

When you *travel,* you go from one place to another.

a b c d e f g h i j k l m

treasure
(treasures)

Treasure is gold, silver and precious jewels.

tree
(trees)

A *tree* is a tall plant with a trunk made of wood. It has branches and leaves on it.

triangle
(triangles)

A *triangle* is a flat shape with three sides and three corners.

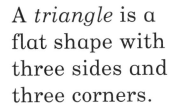

trick
(tricks)

A *trick* is a clever thing to do to entertain people.

trouble
(troubles)

Trouble is something that makes people upset or worries you.

trousers

Trousers are a piece of clothing that cover your legs and the lower part of your body.

truck
(trucks)

A *truck* is a kind of lorry.

tuck
(tucks, tucking, tucked)

1. When you *tuck* something in, you tidy the loose ends away.
2. If you *tuck* someone in at bedtime, you make sure they are warm and comfortable with the bedclothes all around them.

tug-of-war
(tugs-of-war)

A *tug-of-war* is a competition between two teams who pull on a big rope to see which team is the strongest.

turn
(turns, turning, turned)

1. When you *turn*, you move to face a different way.
2. When it is your *turn* to do something, it is your go.

turnip
(turnips)

A *turnip* is a round, white vegetable that grows underground.

a b c d e f g h i j k l m

turtle
(turtles)

A *turtle* is a large sea creature with a thick shell.

TV
(TVs)

see television

twig
(twigs)

A *twig* is a tiny branch on a tree or a bush.

twist
(twists, twisting, twisted)

If you *twist* something, you turn one part of it to face a different direction.

type
(types)

A *type* of something is the sort that it is.

n o p q r s **t** u v w x y z

171

ugly
(uglier, ugliest)

Someone who is *ugly* is not pleasant to look at.

uncle
(uncles)

Your *uncle* is the brother of your father or mother.

underground

Underground means under the ground.

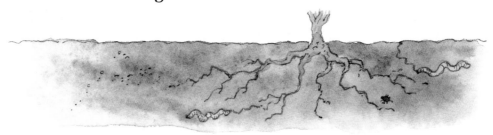

uniform
(uniforms)

A *uniform* is a special set of clothes that people wear to show the job that they do or the school that they go to.

use
(uses, using, used)

If you *use* something like a tool, you do something with it to help you.

a b c d e f g h i j k l m

V v

van
(vans)

A *van* is a small covered truck for carrying things from place to place.

vegetable
(vegetables)

A *vegetable* is a plant which is eaten raw or cooked. Potatoes, cabbage and beans are *vegetables*.

vehicle
(vehicles)

A *vehicle* is anything that takes people from one place to another. Cars, vans, buses, carts and lorries are all *vehicles*.

village
(villages)

A *village* is a small group of houses in the country. There is often a church, a shop and a pub.

voice
(voices)

Your *voice* is the sound you make when you speak or sing.

wagon
(wagons)

A *wagon* is a strong cart with four wheels that a farmer uses to move heavy loads. It is often pulled by horses or oxen.

wait
(waits, waiting, waited)

If you *wait*, you spend some time before anything happens or before you can do anything.

wake
(wakes, waking, woke, woken)

When you *wake up*, you stop being asleep.

WAKE UP!

walk
(walks, walking, walked)

1. When you *walk*, you put one foot in front of the other to move along.
2. A *walk* is a journey on foot.

wall
(walls)

1. A *wall* is used to divide two pieces of land. It is usually made of bricks or stone.

2. A *wall* is one side of a room.

walrus
(walruses)

A *walrus* is an animal that lives in the sea. It looks like a big seal. It has long tusks and a hairy face. *Walruses* usually come from the Arctic.

wand
(wands)

A magician uses a *wand* to make magic spells work.

war
(wars)

A *war* is a fight between countries that may go on for a long time.

warden
(wardens)

A *warden* looks after something, like a block of flats or a road crossing.

wardrobe
(wardrobes)

A *wardrobe* is a tall cupboard where you can hang your clothes.

warm
(warmer, warmest)

A *warm* place is almost hot.

warn
(warns, warning, warned)

If you *warn* someone, you tell them that they are in danger.

wash
(washes, washing, washed)

1. When you *wash*, you use water and soap to clean yourself.
2. If you *wash* clothes, you clean them with water and soap and hang them to dry on a *washing line*.

a b c d e f g h i j k l m

watch
(watches,
watching,
watched)

1. If you *watch* something, you look at it for a long time.
2. When you call '*Watch out!*', you warn someone of danger.

water
(waters,
watering,
watered)

1. *Water* is a clear liquid that falls from the sky as rain and flows in rivers to the sea.
2. If you *water* a plant, you pour water on it to help it grow.

wave
(waves, waving,
waved)

1. A *wave* is a line of water that moves on the sea.
2. If you *wave*, you move your hand in the air to say goodbye or hello to someone.

wear
(wears, wearing,
wore, worn)

When you *wear* clothes, you have them on your body.

weather

Weather is what it is like outside each day. Rain, snow, sun, fog and wind are all part of the weather.

web
(webs)

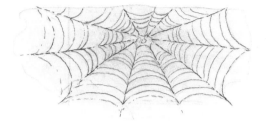

A *web* is a thin net that spiders make to catch their prey.

weed
(weeds)

A *weed* is a wild plant that grows where you do not want it to grow.

week
(weeks)

A *week* is seven days.

weight
(weights)

The *weight* of something is how heavy it is.

well
(wells; better, best)

1. A *well* is a deep hole in the ground which has been dug to reach water.
2. If something grows *well*, it gets *better* and better.
3. If you sleep *well*, you have a good sleep.

wet
(wetter, wettest)

If something or someone is *wet*, they are covered with liquid.

a b c d e f g h i j k l m

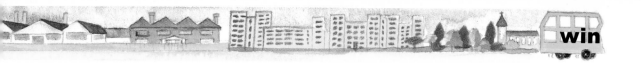
whale
(whales)

A *whale* is the largest sea animal there is.

whole
(wholes)

The *whole* of something is all of it.

wide
(wider, widest)

Something *wide* measures a long way from side to side.

wild
(wilder, wildest)

Wild animals live in the fields, jungles and forests. They are not used to living with people.

win
(wins, winning, won)

If you *win* a race or a competition, you come first.

wind
(winds)

Wind is air that is moving across the earth.

window
(windows)

A *window* is a sheet of glass across a hole in the wall that lets in the light.

wise
(wiser, wisest)

Someone who is *wise* knows many things.

witch
(witches)

In fairy stories, a *witch* is a woman who uses magic. *Witches* fly on broomsticks and wear long pointed hats.

woke

see wake

a b c d e f g h i j k l m

wolf
(wolves)

A *wolf* is a wild animal that looks like a large dog.

woman
(women)

A *woman* is a girl who has grown up.

wombat
(wombats)

A *wombat* is a small furry animal that lives in Australia. *Wombats* eat plants.

wonder
(wonders,
wondering,
wondered)

If you *wonder* about something, you think about it and want to know more.

wool
(wools)

Wool is the thick, soft hair that grows on sheep. It can be spun, woven or knitted and then used for making clothes.

word
(words)

A *word* is a sound that you say, write or read, and that you understand.

wore

see wear

work
(works, working, worked)

When you *work*, you are busy doing something. Many people get paid for *working*.

world
(worlds)

The *world* is the planet we live on.

worm
(worms)

A *worm* is a long, thin creature that lives in the soil. *Worms* have no bones and no legs.

worn

see wear

wound
(wounds, wounding, wounded)

1. A *wound* is a cut or a hole in someone's flesh.
2. If someone is *wounded*, they are hurt.

a b c d e f g h i j k l m

wriggle
(wriggles,
wriggling,
wriggled)

When you *wriggle*, you twist and turn your body very quickly. You are *wriggly*.

wrinkle
(wrinkles)

A *wrinkle* is a small line in the skin.

write
(writes, writing,
wrote, written)

When you *write*, you make marks or words on paper so that people can read them.

wrong

If you are *wrong*, you are not right.

X-ray
(X-rays)

An *X-ray* is a special photograph that shows the inside of the body.

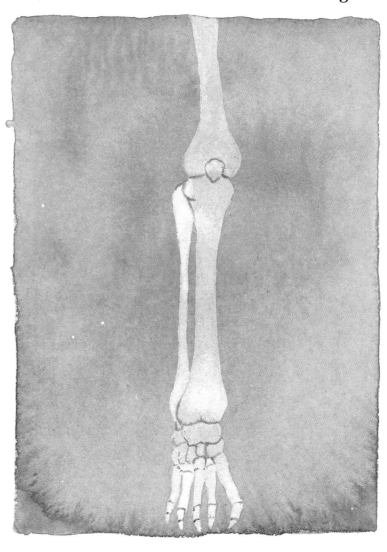

a b c d e f g h i j k l m

yawn
(yawns, yawning, yawned)

When you *yawn*, you open your mouth wide and breathe in more air. You yawn because you are tired.

year
(years)

A *year* is a length of time which lasts for twelve months.

young
(younger, youngest)

A *young* person, animal or plant has not lived very long.

Numbers

1	one	9	nine
2	two	10	ten
3	three	11	eleven
4	four	12	twelve
5	five	13	thirteen
6	six	14	fourteen
7	seven	15	fifteen
8	eight	16	sixteen

last

fifth

fourth

17	seventeen	50	fifty
18	eighteen	60	sixty
19	nineteen	70	seventy
20	twenty	80	eighty
21	twenty-one	90	ninety
22	twenty-two	100	one hundred
30	thirty	1 000	one thousand
40	forty	1 000 000	one million

third

second

FINISH

first

Position words and colours

purple

pink

white

above

below

on

blue

against

188

black

grey

green

orange

red

up

brown

yellow

beside

down

inside

between

outside

over

in front of

behind

under

189

Seasons and months

Winter

December   January   February

Autumn

September   October   November

190

March   April   May

Summer

June   July   August

191

Days of the week

Sneeze on Monday, sneeze for danger;
Sneeze on Tuesday, meet a stranger;
Sneeze on Wednesday, get a letter;
Sneeze on Thursday, something better;
Sneeze on Friday, sneeze for sorrow;
Sneeze on Saturday, see your
    sweetheart tomorrow.

Question words

Who... ?
What... ?
When... ?
Why... ?
How... ?
Where... ?
Which... ?
Whose... ?